The Eloquent Mindset

**Enhance Public Speaking Skills,
Maximize Personal Impact ,
Boost Confidence, Influence, and
Charisma for Superior Communication**

Manjul Tewari

www.manjultewari.com

"I found this book really helpful in overcoming my nervousness when speaking in front of groups at work. The practical exercises gave me specific techniques to practice rather than just telling me to be confident like other public speaking books. I especially appreciated the section on storytelling that showed me how to structure my presentation to keep the audience engaged instead of just listing facts and information."

—Stacy Gragnani

"This is a deep book whose wisdom is easily accessible, laying out the real principles and techniques for effective public communication. It is clear, well-written, well-organized, and gives practical insights for those uneasy with public oratory. Highly recommended!"

—Daniel B. Lyle

"The author explains very simply and clearly how to build self-confidence through the ability to convey your thoughts. I especially remember the chapter on 'unshakable charisma'—for the first time someone explained how to be yourself and at the same time be heard. A calm, smart, and sincere book."

—**Daria Chyzhykova**

Published by **Mr. Manjul Tewari**
P-24, Engineer Park Apartment, Omega Sector-1
Greater Noida, UP, India 201308

To My Parents

CONTENTS

INTRODUCTION

Do you know what people fear more than death? Speaking in infront of an audience.

It sounds absurd at first, but studies show that nearly 75% of people suffer from glossophobia—the crippling fear of public speaking. Your palms sweat. Your heart races. Your voice trembles. Suddenly, the brilliant ideas in your head vanish the moment you step into the spotlight.

I remember a young software engineer named Rohan who came to me after one of my workshops. He was brilliant at his job—his ideas had saved his company both time and money—yet when asked to present his project to the senior leadership team, he froze. His mind went blank, words stumbled out in fragments, and the confidence he felt in front of his laptop evaporated in front of an audience. Later, he told me, "I would rather code for 16 hours straight than speak for 16 minutes on stage."

Does that sound familiar? Perhaps you've felt the same. You prepare endlessly, you rehearse your lines, but the moment you stand up, your nerves betray you. The audience doesn't see the depth of your knowledge; they only see hesitation, awkward pauses, and shaky delivery. And you walk away, frustrated, thinking, "Why can't I just speak the way I think?"

Yet here's the truth: communication isn't optional anymore. In today's hyper-connected world, it's the skill that determines leadership, influence, and success. The ability to speak with clarity and impact can open doors that talent and technical knowledge alone cannot. You might have the best ideas in the room, but if you cannot present them with conviction, someone else—often less qualified—will take the spotlight.

That's why I wrote The Eloquent Mindset. This book isn't just about learning to give speeches. It's about transforming yourself from anxious and hesitant to confident and captivating.

Why Words Matter So Much

Think about history's greatest leaders: Gandhi, Martin Luther King Jr., Churchill, Kennedy, and Mandela. What did they all have in common? They understood the power of words. Their voices shaped nations, inspired revolutions, and gave hope in moments of despair.

But this power isn't reserved for politicians or world leaders. Words have the power to win a job interview, persuade a client, calm a restless team, or inspire your child. In every setting—professional, personal, or social—communication is the bridge between your ideas and the world. Without that bridge, your brilliance stays locked inside you.

I've seen it time and again: people far less intelligent or creative succeed simply because they knew how to speak well. They weren't necessarily smarter; they were simply heard. And in a noisy world, being heard is everything.

The Problem with How We Approach Speaking

Most of us were never taught how to communicate effectively. Schools teach math, science, and history, but rarely do they teach the science of rhetoric—the art of persuasion and eloquence. At best, we are told to "speak clearly" or "make eye contact." But when nerves strike, those generic tips feel useless.

So we stumble through trial and error, hoping to "get better with practice." But practice without guidance often reinforces bad habits: monotonous tone, cluttered slides, and rushed delivery. It's no wonder stage fright persists.

The good news? Public speaking is not a gift reserved for a lucky few. It is a learnable skill. Like playing an instrument or mastering a sport, it requires techniques, practice, and the right mindset. With the proper tools, you can transform stage fright into stage readiness.

A Personal Anecdote: My Point

Let me share a story from my own life. Years ago, I was invited to deliver a keynote address at a conference. I had spoken before in smaller settings, but this time, the audience was larger and filled with accomplished professionals.

As I stood backstage, I could feel my chest tighten. My thoughts raced: What if I forget my lines? What if they find me boring? My hands were cold, and my legs felt like stone. I was tempted to walk away.

But then, I remembered something a mentor once told me: "Public speaking is not about you—it's about your audience. Stop obsessing over yourself and start focusing on what value you can give."

That shift changed everything. When I walked on stage, I didn't aim to be perfect. I aimed to connect. I began with a relatable story, spoke with honesty, and paid attention to the energy in the room. The audienceleaned in. They laughed when I laughed. They nodded when I made key points. By the end, not only did I receive applause, but several people approached me saying, "That message was exactly what I needed."

That day, I realized something powerful: eloquence is not about flawless delivery. It's about authentic connection.

What You Will Gain from This Book

Inside The Eloquent Mindset, you'll discover how to:
Turn stage fright into stage confidence by channeling nervous energy into strength.
Captivate any audience with storytelling that sparks emotion and curiosity.
Build presence and charisma so people listen, remember, and act on your words.

Master persuasion to influence with integrity in both personal and professional life.

Craft clear, impactful messages that stick in people's minds long after you've finished speaking.

These aren't abstract theories. They are proven methodsdrawn from psychology, neuroscience, and the timeless practices of history'sgreatest communicators.

The Transformational Power Ideas

Every time you speak, you are planting an idea into another person's mind. When planted well, that idea can inspire action, shift perspectives, and even alter the course of someone's life.

Think of Martin Luther King Jr.'s words: "I have a dream." Just four simple words—but they carried the weight of a vision so powerful that it reshaped society.

On a smaller scale, imagine presenting your project idea clearly to your boss, and it leads to a promotion. Or sharing a heartfelt story with your child, and it shapes the way they see themselves. That is the power of eloquence: small moments that create lasting impact.

Your Journey Starts Here

So here's the truth:

You can let stage fright keep holding you back.

Or you can master the art of eloquence and change the way the world sees you.

If you've ever felt that your voice didn't matter or that your ideas weren't being heard, this book is for you.

The Eloquent Mindset will equip you with the skills, strategies, and mindset to step into the spotlight with confidence. More importantly, it will help you communicate in a way that leaves a lasting legacy.

Because your voice matters.

Your ideas matter.

And it's time the world hears them.

CHAPTER ONE

THE FOUNDATIONS OF ELOQUENT MINDSET

UNDERSTANDING THE IMPORTANCE OF CLEAR AND PERSUASIVE EXPRESSION

"SPEECH IS POWER: SPEECH is to persuade, to convert, to compel. "
- Ralph Waldo Emerson.

Eloquent Mindset serves as the bedrock of human interaction, influencing relationships, businesses, and every facet of society. Consider, for instance, the power of a well-delivered speech, capable of mobilizing entire nations toward a common cause. Similarly, ponder the impact of a misinterpreted text message leading to unnecessary misunderstandings between friends.

These everyday scenarios underscore the importance of comprehending the essentials of effective communication in both personal and professional contexts.

So, what truly constitutes the foundation of effective communication? At its core, effective communication hinges on the art of conveying messages clearly, concisely, and with impact. It involves the seamless transfer of thoughts and ideas from one mind to another, fostering mutual understanding and harmony.

Moreover, effective communication thrives on the pillars of active listening, empathetic understanding, and the adept use of nonverbal cues. Consider the following elements as the building blocks for effective communication:

- **<u>Clarity and Conciseness:</u>**

Expressing thoughts in a clear and straightforward manner ensures that the intended message is comprehensible to the recipient without any ambiguity. Clear communication minimizes the scope for misunderstandings and promotes a shared understanding of the subject matter.

- **<u>Active Listening:</u>** In the sphere of effective communication, listening holds as much significance as articulating one's thoughts. By attentively comprehending the perspectives of others, individuals can foster meaningful dialogues and cultivate a deeper understanding of different viewpoints, thus facilitating effective and empathetic responses.

Empathy and Emotional Intelligence: Understanding the emotions and perspectives of the interlocutor forms the crux of empathetic communication. Acknowledging the emotional nuances underlying a conversation allows for a more compassionate and nuanced response, nurturing trust and fostering stronger interpersonal relationships.

- **<u>Nonverbal Communication</u>:** Beyond spoken words, nonverbal cues such as facial expressions, gestures, and tone of voice play a pivotal role in communicating intent and emotion. By aligning nonverbal cues with verbal communication, individuals can reinforce the intended message and establish a genuine connection with the audience.

Understanding the importance of clear and persuasive expression stands as an indispensable facet of effective communication. Mastering this skill enables individuals to convey their thoughts persuasively while maintaining clarity and sincerity. Whether it involves a persuasive sales pitch, a compelling argument, or a heartfelt conversation, the art of clear and persuasive expression hinges on several key principles:

- **Authenticity**: Authentic expression fosters trust and credibility, enabling individuals to resonate with their audience on a deeper level. Being genuine and true to oneself establishes an emotional connection, thereby compelling the audience to engage more earnestly with the message being conveyed.

- **Structured Messaging:** Organizing thoughts in a logical and coherent manner enhances the persuasiveness of the message. By structuring the content with a clear introduction, well-supported arguments, and a compelling conclusion, individuals can effectively capture the attention of their audience and leave a lasting impact.

- **<u>Tailored Communication</u>**: Tailoring the message to suit the specific needs and preferences of the audience amplifies the effectiveness of communication. Understanding the demographics, interests, and pain points of the target audience allows for the customization of the message, making it more relatable and compelling.

- **<u>Use of Visual Aids:</u>** Incorporating visual aids such as infographics, images, or presentations can significantly enhance the persuasive power of communication. Visual representations serve as powerful tools to supplement verbal communication, enabling individuals to convey complex information in a more accessible and engaging manner.

By adhering to these foundational principles, even a common person can effectively achieve clear and persuasive expression, thereby enhancing their ability to communicate with impact and influence.

Through the conscious application of these principles in everyday conversations and interactions, individuals can gradually hone their communication skills and foster meaningful connections with those around them.

In essence, effective communication is not merely a tool; it embodies the essence of human connection, serving as the catalyst for mutual understanding, cooperation, and progress within the tapestry of human interactions. Embracing the foundational elements and mastering the art of clear and persuasive expression empowers individuals to navigate the intricate realms of communication with grace, efficacy, and authenticity.

Effective communication plays a vital role in various aspects of everyday life, contributing to successful relationships, businesses, and societal interactions. Here are some real-life examples that illustrate the significance of effective communication:

- **<u>Effective Leadership Communication</u>**: Consider the exemplary communication skills of renowned leaders such as Mahatma Gandhi and Martin Luther King Jr. Their powerful speeches, grounded in empathy, clarity, and a compelling vision, inspired millions to join their movements for social change. Through their effective communication, they were able to unite diverse groups of people under a common cause and drive significant societal transformations.

- **<u>Business Success through Communication</u>**: Think about the success stories of influential entrepreneurs like Steve Jobs. His ability to communicate a compelling vision for Apple's products, combined with his persuasive presentation skills, played a crucial role in the widespread adoption of Apple's innovative technologies. By effectively conveying the value and uniqueness of Apple's products, Jobs fostered a dedicated customer base and solidified Apple's position as a global tech giant.

- **<u>Effective Interpersonal Communication</u>**: Consider a scenario where a couple successfully resolves a conflict through open and empathetic communication. By actively listening to each other's concerns, expressing their thoughts and emotions clearly, and showing understanding and empathy, the couple can reach a mutually satisfactory resolution. This demonstrates how effective communication fosters trust, strengthens emotional bonds, and nurtures healthier and more resilient relationships.

- **International Diplomacy**: Diplomatic relations between countries heavily rely on effective communication. Diplomats and leaders engaging in sensitive negotiations must communicate clearly and diplomatically to reach mutually beneficial agreements. The successful conclusion of significant international treaties and peace accords, such as the Paris Agreement on climate change, exemplifies the power of effective communication in fostering global cooperation and addressing critical issues.

- **Effective Teaching and Learning**: In the educational sphere, effective communication is crucial for teachers to impart knowledge and facilitate meaningful learning experiences for students.

A teacher who can explain complex concepts in a simple and engaging manner, encourage active participation, and provide constructive feedback can significantly enhance students' understanding and academic performance. Such effective communication fosters a positive learning environment and cultivates a passion for learning among students.

These real-life examples underscore the profound impact of effective communication across various domains, emphasizing its role in fostering understanding, building trust, and driving positive change. Whether in the realms of leadership, business, interpersonal relationships, diplomacy, or education, the ability to communicate effectively serves as a cornerstone for success, cooperation, and meaningful human connections.

Key Takeaways:

Importance of Effective Communication:

Effective communication serves as the cornerstone of human interactions, influencing relationships, businesses, and every aspect of society.

It enables the seamless transfer of thoughts and ideas, fostering mutual understanding and harmony in both personal and professional contexts.

Foundational Elements of Effective Communication:

Clarity and Conciseness: Expressing thoughts clearly and straightforwardly minimizes misunderstandings and promotes shared understanding.

Active Listening: Attentively comprehending the perspectives of others fosters meaningful dialogues and a deeper understanding of different viewpoints.

Empathy and Emotional Intelligence: Acknowledging the emotional nuances underlying a conversation allows for a more compassionate and nuanced response, nurturing trust and fostering stronger interpersonal relationships.

Nonverbal Communication: Nonverbal cues such as facial expressions, gestures, and tone of voice play a pivotal role in communicating intent and emotion, reinforcing the intended message and establishing a genuine connection with the audience.

Principles of Clear and Persuasive Expression:

Authenticity: Being genuine and true to oneself fosters trust and credibility, enabling a deeper emotional connection with the audience.

Structured Messaging: Organizing thoughts in a logical and coherent manner enhances the persuasiveness of the message, capturing the audience's attention and leaving a lasting impact.

Tailored Communication: Customizing the message to suit the specific needs and preferences of the audience amplifies the effectiveness of communication, making it more relatable and compelling.

Use of Visual Aids:

Incorporating visual aids such as infographics and presentations enhances the persuasive power of communication, facilitating the conveyance of complex information in an accessible and engaging manner.

Examples of Effective Communication:

Effective Leadership Communication: Exemplary communication skills of leaders like Mahatma Gandhi and Martin Luther King Jr. inspired societal change and unity through powerful speeches grounded in empathy and a compelling vision.

Business Success through Communication: Entrepreneurs like Steve Jobs utilized persuasive communication to convey the value of their products, fostering a dedicated customer base and solidifying their companies' positions in the market.

Effective Interpersonal Communication: Open and empathetic communication fosters trust, strengthens emotional bonds, and resolves conflicts within relationships.

International Diplomacy: Successful international agreements and treaties demonstrate the power of effective communication in fostering global cooperation and addressing critical issues.

Effective Teaching and Learning: Effective communication in education facilitates meaningful learning experiences, simplifying complex concepts and encouraging active participation among students.

These key takeaways highlight the pivotal role of effective communication in various aspects of everyday life, emphasizing its contribution to successful relationships, businesses, and societal interactions. They underscore the importance of clear and persuasive expression, showcasing how mastering these communication skills can empower individuals to navigate the complexities of human interactions with authenticity, efficacy, and grace.

CHAPTER TWO

EFFECTIVE STRATEGIES AND TIPS FOR GAINING CONFIDENCE WHILE SPEAKING PUBLICLY

OVERCOME THE FEAR OF PUBLIC SPEAKING IN ANY SITUATION

"**A**UDIENCE INTERACTION SHOULD BE proportional to the amount of trust you've earned.

-Michael Port

A) Stage Fright

As a child, I had stage fright whenever I was called on stage to recite poetry or a short story in front of an audience. It was primarily due to an incident when I slipped on stage while climbing up the podium stairs. The fellow children laughed and mocked. I could not utter a single word as I froze on stage. It has never been the same after that day. Most people who fear public speaking have traumatic past public speaking experiences and often fear repeating them and becoming a subject of ridicule from the audience. Many people fear public speaking more than they fear death.

My own experience at public speaking was no better. I was too terrified to speak before the audience and tried to do anything to escape the ordeal of public speaking. If public speaking became inevitable, either I would start stammering before the crowd or would freeze without uttering a single word. While growing up as a young man, giving interviews before a handful of people or participating in group discussions also became an arduous task.

Soon, I realized that I would not get cured of this disorder by some divine providence. I knew by then that I would have to learn all the tricks of the trade and master the art of public speaking if I was ready to grab the opportunities coming my way.

Presently I enjoy standing before the crowd and telling stories, giving impromptu speeches that are pretty appreciated, hosting in media training centres and electronic media talk shows. In one of my part-time assignments, I taught a group of fifty students the basics of communication as a guest faculty. I have also successfully faced interview boards and participated in group discussions where I have put forth my point of view convincingly.

B) The Transformation

An incident that had a profound impact on my public speaking was when one of the star campaigners of the local public representative visited our community some four years ago. After his inspiring speech, he encouraged the audience to share ideas for more extensive public participation in civic matters. While I had a good idea of what I wanted to convey, I was too scared to stand up and give my opinion; I got my perspective from a friend standing beside me. Hearing my concept, he immediately went on stage and presented it before the audience. Something I was too scared to do.

The star speaker hearing the concept was too happy and hugely complimented my friend. I was both angry with myself yet delighted that my idea was welcomed.

I was disappointed with myself and thought of finding a solution to this problem and ultimately overcoming this issue.

Besides, I was getting nowhere in my interviews to secure a steady job as I could not express myself before the interview board, although I was doing well in written tests. It was that time when I decided that enough was enough, and I would do anything and everything required to conquer my fear of speaking in public.

I started reading all that came my way on public speaking and how to conquer the fear of speaking and watched all excellent speakers on the internet. Gradually by sheer experimentations and genuine attempts to acquire this new skill and learning what works best for me, I started observing small steps initially to prepare myself to speak my mind coherently and explicitly in front of the crowd.

C) Baby steps

Not wanting to feel belittled before my well-wishers and friends who would breeze through any public speaking event, I decided to pull up my sleeves and do well even on those occasions where I was addressing a huge crowd.

I even took the help of a professional counsellor to provide much-needed mental strengch.

The counsellor offered some valuable tips, asking me initially not to look towards the audience while speaking. He also suggested I see what works best for me in given situations as no two people may face the same set of problems. There's no point in comparing myself to someone who doesn't have the same issue. I thought about solutions that best suited me while facing the audience. So, I dedicated myself to finding ways to take the first few steps. And one by one, I started prioritizing certain practices, which I began to pursue before every occasion when I had to speak publicly.

D) Before the day

Step 1: Get acquainted with the location

Whenever possible, I try to see the place where I have to speak one day before the actual event. I take a stroll around the venue and get to know the area, feeling the people who would be before me while I speak on the day of the event. I get a fair idea about what to expect to improve my performance.

Step 2: Writing the speech

It is even better to write down the salient points of your speech by hand and not resort to typing the entire script. I would be armed with this vital piece of paper, while practicing the presentation. It is generally found that writing the script with hand, even empowers you with greater confidence. It gives me a different kind of reassurance in knowing that I had written the speech while also noticing the errors and edits.

Recent research has shown that we process the given information more deeply if we write the matter. The confidence level builds up seeing the self-written speech with corrections and edits. Research has shown that writing things down on paper helps in more profoundly processing the information and building up self-assurance.

Step 3: Practicing before the mirror in a complete outfit.

I dread facing the scenario where I am the laughing stock of the audience and disappointing them with a below-par performance. I feel unsure of my voice, I feel self-conscious of my accent, pose, gesture, and attire. In these circumstances, I have found the mirror gives the best assessment. Invariably I finish my presentation at least two days before the appointed day while practising before the mirror as much as I can. The practice session before the mirror would also include two sessions with full outfits that I plan to wear on the presentation day.

These practice sessions in front of the mirror greatly assist me in looking at my poise, accent, gestures to figure out everything from how I stand, how I smile and how I gesticulate. These sessions also make me stress-free to quite an extent as I know what I will say, how I will smile, how I am going to stand. That's the way I choose to remain confident, focused, and secure in my thoughts.

Step 4: Doing a mock-up presentation before friends and family members just before the actual day, whom I trust and who give their honest feedback on some of the essential elements such as where to pause, where to go for high pitch, and seek clarifications and give advice as to how to better my presentation. This technique helps me prepare for any unscripted portion of the presentation or interview.

E) On the day

Step 1: I arrive at the venue early. I want to avoid the dreadful thought of addressing the crowd after arriving late for the speech-making event, with no preparation and getting tongue-tied at the beginning of the speech itself. I invariably arrive one to two hours early to avoid this dreadful scenario. It allows me to recollect all that I have to say mentally. And if the room or the venue is unfamiliar to me, I would walk and take a look around to get the feel of the place.

Besides, arriving early also has other pros, like getting my laptop tuned in with the projection system, which gives me additional confidence.

Additional time also gives me a window to talk to other speakers present and chit-chat with the backstage technical crew members to acquaint myself with the scene.

Step 2: Trying to stay relaxed

Just before the event is about to begin, my heart begins to accelerate its beat. At times even my head starts swinging around, and I can't think of anything. Those speakers who are new to this are sitting beside me, and having the same edginess appears to push me further towards the hill. I try to find some space away from all this and relax by taking a long, deep, and slow breath.

Hence the last hour before my public speaking event, I try not to look at the script and limit myself controlling my breath and keeping my nervousness in check.

Step 3: Be the first speaker, if possible

There are chances that the long wait can result in anxiety and apprehension.

If I am required to wait for my turn and listen to others' speeches, the possibilities are that I may forget what I have to say altogether due to the built-up nervousness level. While waiting, for my turn and keeping my fingers crossed for an unknown outcome of my presentation, can only increase my panic level. Hence, given a possibility or a choice, I request the organizers to speak first before the others.

Speaking first and before others help me stay focused on what I have to say without judging myself by others' performance.

Step 4: Speak with pauses.

My main worry is to avoid nervousness while speaking. At times my mouth dries up, my jaw drops, and my throat chokes up due to stage fright. If that happens, it is quite a task for me to bounce back into the speech and still make a good impression.

I take a slight pause after two and three sentences to avoid this. While this gives me a window space to recollect my thoughts while taking a deep breath, it allows the audience to understand the chain of ideas coming from me. Recent studies have shown that pauses depict a more truthful interpretation of facts, making it more genuine hence more interesting.

I always keep a water bottle that helps me take a water break every fifteen minutes, especially when taking classes with students.

Step 5: Talking in small, precise sentences

Another method to not get too anxious is to talk in small but accurate sentences. Long sentences should be avoided at any cost. It indeed makes me forget what I was speaking about. And the audience will also loose track of what you are saying. To remain on track, lest I forget what I was talking about, I also keep a card with salient points written about my speech. It helps me stay on track with my remarks.

While presenting from a laptop, I always keep a card or a piece of paper to write down the presentation's main points. Though earlier I used to read the entire speech on paper, I have now gained confidence in keeping the main points noted on a piece of paper after steady practice.

Step 6: Not focusing on people's faces

Studies have revealed that making eye contact is an essential element that helps the speech become memorable. But when I looked into people's eyes while speaking before a large crowd, I would forget my lines and begin to think about what the person in the audience was thinking of my speech. I would start to have apprehensions that they are either bored or are annoyed about what I have just said. It would further trigger anxiety and nervousness. It was another factor for my fear of speaking in public.

But by some trials and error method, it soon dawned on me that if I do not look into the eyes of someone directly and, on the other hand, give the impression of looking into the faces of the audience, then it would appear that I am talking to them. While I am not staring into the audience's eyes, it gives me relief as I cannot find out their expressions. And I keep rotating the focus of my glance back and forth into the audience without looking individually at anyone in particular.

Step 7: Preparing for Impromptu Speeches

Small family gatherings are the best occasions for making short impromptu speeches where one can practice speaking in public without fear of being in an awkward situation.

Initially, I was even scared to speak in family gatherings. However, our family gatherings usually are occasions when all youngsters are allowed to speak out their minds. But again, I was petrified about what they would think about me.

However, I was encouraged to speak my mind in the family gatherings. Because even if I choked with emotion or would stammer due to fear of getting the attention, I would not be too bothered as, after all, it was only a family gathering.

Step 8 : It helped when I accepted my awkwardness.

When I face many naughty students in a classroom while teaching, it helps me discover my shortcomings to a greater extent, I soon realize that I am not too confident when I address them. This realization has, for some time, helped me reduce my anxiety level.

Hence, I accept at the very beginning of any impromptu speech that I am not very good at being in the limelight and do not have any prior preparation. In casual gatherings, this honest acceptance has eased my nervousness to some level.

There is every possibility that the majority of those listening would themselves not be too good in making public speeches. Hence there is a chance that the "imperfect audience" may be more forgiving and would accept me sympathetically as a speaker. Thus, the audience's fear of examining me too closely on my content and style and laughing and ridiculing me seems to have less probability.

Step 9: Making jokes at your expense will have the audience slightly more accepting.

Minor mistakes do inevitably occur during long speeches. And those who are more sensitive to their criticism can hear some of the audience passing comments or a giggle, which is enough to derail your chain of thought, leading to a further increase in anxiety level. An occasional joke cracked at your own expense would trigger a positive audience response. It lightens up the mood in general and creates a fun atmosphere. For example, if I ever face an awkward situation in front of a room full of people before a speech, I dare to laugh it off, saying, "That was choreographed," or "I fell harder than I intended after all." Such remarks would remove any traces of humiliation in their minds while turning it into a joke and can start all over it again with a clean slate.

Step 10: Believe in what you say

If the topic is selected judiciously, half the battle is won already. If the chosen topic is close to my heart and I firmly believe in it and cherish sharing the idea with others, then the speech would be a cakewalk and trouble-free and may also stir up emotional support from the audience.

Once I was attending an inter-college debating event where the negative fallout of technology and modern culture on youth was being discussed. The organizers announced from the stage that they were looking for volunteer speakers from the audience who would speak on the given topic without any preparation.

The event was a big one, and I, mustering all the courage signed up to be one of the volunteer speakers. It was a huge event, but still, I gathered my nerves to sign up as a speaker. I went to the stage and talked about the adverse effects of social media sites as I knew someone who had suffered hugely from such networking sites. I had jotted specific points on a piece of paper and written certain figures and factual data related to the topic. I spoke for 30 minutes, which even I didn't expect. I made a mark that day and impressed the people who even gave me a prize for my speech. But above all, I was hugely happy with myself for bringing glory to myself. The credit for delivering a resounding speech mainly had gone to the fact that the topic was very dear to me, and I spoke from the core of the heart believing in every word that I spoke that day.

Key Take Away

1. Overcome the fear of public speaking in any situation

   a. Show confidence, believe that you are telling the audience something new

   b. Laughing with the audience is better than being laughed at

   c. Lose the fear of disapproval

   d. Self-acceptance of ourselves is key to fighting out and overcoming speech nervousness.

   e. Make a written statement of all the significant points of the speech.

   f. Practice well before the event

g. Select the topic judiciously, something you are passionate about

h. Have an appreciative attitude towards yourself

i. Fully understand your shortcomings

2. Before the day

a. Get acquainted with the location

b. Writing the speech

c. Have a look at the place where you have to speak before the event

d. Write down the salient points of your speech by hand

e. Practicing before the mirror in a complete outfit as it gives the best assessment

f. Doing a mock-up presentation before friends and family members

3. **On the day**

a. Arrive at the venue early

b. Trying to stay relaxed

c. Be the first speaker, if possible

d. Speak with pauses

e. Talking in small, precise sentences

f. Not focusing on people's faces

4. Preparing for impromptu speeches

5.It helps when you accept your awkwardness
6.Making jokes at your expense will move the audience to be more accepting
7.Believe in what you say

CHAPTER FOUR

MASTERING THE ART OF STORYTELLING AND ENGAGING YOUR AUDIENCE

CRAFTING A STRONG NARRATIVE

"IF YOU'RE NOT COMFORTABLE **with public speaking - and nobody starts comfortable; you have to learn how to be comfortable - practice. I cannot overstate the importance of practicing. Get some close friends or family members to help evaluate you, or somebody at work that you trust."**
-Hillary Clinton.

Mastering the art of storytelling is an incredible skill that has the power to captivate an audience, ignite their imagination, and leave a lasting impression. I've discovered that weaving a compelling narrative isn't just about the sequence of events; it's about creating an emotional connection and painting a vivid picture that resonates with the audience. Here's how I've learned to master this art, along with some personal examples to illustrate the process.

First and foremost, I always begin by understanding my audience. Knowing their interests, experiences, and expectations allows me to tailor my story to their preferences. For instance, during a recent book reading event, I noticed that the audience was particularly fond of adventure tales. So, I shared a personal anecdote about a thrilling hiking expedition I embarked on in the Himalayas. I described the breathtaking scenery, the challenges I faced, and the lessons I learned, which instantly captured their attention and created a sense of shared experience.

Crafting a strong narrative structure is equally important. I structure my s tories to have a clear beginning, middle, and end. This framework helps to build anticipation and maintain the audience's engagement throughout the storytelling journey. I recall a time when I was recounting my travel experiences across Europe. I started by setting the scene in a bustling Parisian café, then delved into the various adventures and mishaps that unfolded during my trip, and finally, I concluded with a reflection on the profound impact the journey had on my perspective.

Injecting emotions into the narrative is key to fostering a deep connection with the audience . I make sure to convey not only the events but also the feelings associated with them. For instance, when narrating a heartwarming incident about volunteering at a local shelter, I vividly expressed the joy and fulfillment I experienced while interacting with the rescued animals. This emotional touch not only resonated with the audience's compassion but also evoked a sense of shared empathy and understanding.

Adding relatable characters and relaying their experiences is another technique I use to make my stories more engaging. By introducing individuals with whom the audience can empathize, I create a more immersive and relatable narrative. During a recent talk on the challenges of entrepreneurship, I introduced a character based on my own experiences - an ambitious young entrepreneur navigating the complexities of starting a business. Sharing the character's struggles, triumphs, and personal growth enabled the audience to connect with the broader theme of perseverance and determination.

Using descriptive language and sensory details is crucial in painting a vivid picture for the audience. I often incorporate colorful imagery, evocative language, and sensory descriptions to bring the settings and experiences to life. When narrating a cultural festival I attended in India, I described the vibrant decorations, the rhythmic beats of traditional music, and the aroma of local delicacies, allowing the audience to immerse themselves in the cultural richness of the event.

Seamlessly incorporating suspense and surprise elements into the narrative keeps the audience on the edge of their seats. I recall a time when I shared a personal story about a serendipitous encounter during a solo trip. By gradually building up the suspense and revealing unexpected twists, I heightened the audience's curiosity and anticipation, making the story all the more memorable and engaging.

Lastly, I always emphasize the power of a meaningful takeaway. Every story should convey a valuable lesson, a moral, or an insight that resonates with the audience long after the narrative has concluded. During a recent workshop on resilience, I shared a personal story of overcoming professional setbacks, emphasizing the importance of perseverance and self-belief. By illustrating the transformative power of resilience, I aimed to inspire the audience to approach challenges with a positive mindset and unwavering determination.

In conclusion, mastering the art of storytelling and engaging the audience isn't just about narrating events; it's about creating an immersive experience that resonates with the audience on an emotional level. By understanding the audience, crafting a compelling narrative structure, infusing emotions, introducing relatable characters, employing descriptive language, incorporating suspense, and emphasizing valuable takeaways, I've found that I can effectively capture the hearts and minds of my listeners and leave a lasting impact through the power of storytelling.

Strategies for Captivating and Holding Attention

In an era inundated with ceaseless distractions and an incessant barrage of information, capturing and maintaining an audience's attention has become an arduous challenge. Whether you're a seasoned writer, a burgeoning entrepreneur, or a content creator striving to make an impact, understanding the intricacies of holding attention is crucial.

Capturing and maintaining my audience's attention has been an exhilarating yet challenging journey. As an independent author based in the bustling city of New Delhi, India, I've come to realize that understanding my readers is the cornerstone of my craft. When I published my first book, a collection of short stories, I delved deep into my readers' preferences and found that they were drawn to emotionally evocative narratives. Taking this insight to heart, I meticulously crafted characters and plots that mirrored their daily struggles and triumphs, effectively captivating their attention from the very first page.

The ability to captivate an audience is an art, blending a profound understanding of human psychology with effective communication strategies. Here we will aim to dissect and explore a myriad of approaches and techniques that can help you master the craft of engaging your audience, ensuring that your message is not just heard but truly resonates.

Understanding Your Audience:

Before embarking on any creative endeavor, it is imperative to comprehend your target audience. Take time to research their preferences, interests, and pain points. By empathizing with their needs and desires, you can tailor your content to speak directly to them. This understanding forms the foundation upon which you can build a captivating narrative that resonates with your readers.

According to a recent survey conducted by the Content Marketing Institute, 67% of consumers reported that they preferred personalized content that addressed their specific needs and interests. This underscores the significance of tailoring content to meet the preferences of the target audience.

Compelling Narrative Structure:

Storytelling remains a powerful tool for captivating an audience. Craft a narrative that unfolds organically, balancing anticipation and resolution. Engage your readers by introducing relatable characters, conflicts, and a compelling plot that evokes emotional resonance. Employ the art of suspense and surprise to maintain a gripping storyline, keeping your audience on the edge of their seats.

Visual Appeal and Multimedia Integration:

In my recent work, a travel memoir chronicling my adventures through the picturesque landscapes of the Himalayas, I understood the power of visual storytelling. By integrating captivating images of the snow-capped peaks and serene valleys, I didn't just narrate my experiences but allowed my readers to vicariously immerse themselves in the breathtaking beauty I had encountered. The inclusion of multimedia elements transformed my narrative into a vivid tapestry, fostering a more profound connection with my audience.

A study by HubSpot revealed that articles with images receive 94% more views than those without. Furthermore, incorporating videos in content marketing has been shown to increase website traffic by up to 55%. This emphasizes the pivotal role of visual content in capturing and maintaining audience engagement.

Incorporate visually appealing elements such as striking images, infographics, and videos to complement your textual content. Visual stimuli have the potency to seize attention swiftly and enhance comprehension. Utilize multimedia platforms to provide a holistic and engaging experience that transcends the confines of traditional text-based communication.

Engaging Headlines and Introductions:

Crafting attention-grabbing headlines has been a game-changer for me. In my book discussing the intricacies of self-publishing, I employed thought-provoking questions in my introduction to hook my readers. By posing queries like "Ever dreamed of sharing your story with the world? Let's embark on this journey together," I immediately sparked their curiosity, encouraging them to explore the comprehensive insights I had to offer.

Research by Outbrain indicates that 8 out of 10 individuals read a headline, while only 2 out of 10 proceed to read the entire article. This highlights the critical importance of compelling headlines in capturing initial attention and enticing readers to explore the full content.

The initial moments of interaction are crucial. Craft attention-grabbing headlines and introductions that pique curiosity and compel readers to delve deeper into your content. Employ rhetoric, intriguing questions, or thought-provoking statements to create an immediate connection and entice your audience to stay invested.

Emotional Resonance and Empathy:

Connect with your audience on an emotional level. Foster empathy by addressing their concerns, aspirations, and fears. Relatable and authentic content that taps into shared human experiences fosters a sense of belonging and encourages readers to invest emotionally in your message.

<u>**Interactivity and Engagement:**</u>

I've also come to understand the significance of fostering a sense of community through interactive engagement. During the virtual launch of my latest book, I organized a live Q&A session where readers could share their thoughts and ask me questions. This interactive exchange not only deepened their engagement with my work but also fostered a sense of belonging within a community of like-minded individuals passionate about literature and travel.

According to a report by Salesforce, 64% of consumers and 80% of business buyers expect real-time interaction. Additionally, content that encourages user participation, such as polls and surveys, has been found to increase engagement rates by 65%, as reported by Content Marketing Institute.

Foster a sense of community by encouraging active engagement and participation. Initiate discussions, polls, and interactive sessions that invite readers to contribute their thoughts and perspectives. Create a feedback loop that not only acknowledges but also incorporates the voices of your audience, making them feel valued and heard.

<u>**Incorporating Humor and Wit:**</u>

Incorporating humor into my writing has not only enlivened my content but also forged an intimate bond with my readers. In one of my travelogues, I shared a humorous anecdote about my encounter with a mischievous monkey in Rishikesh, a picturesque town at the foothills of Himalayas in the northern part of India, which left my readers chuckling and eager for more delightful tales from my sojourn. The infusion of wit has served as a refreshing tonic, allowing my audience to connect with me on a more personal and light-hearted level.

A study published in the Journal of Marketing found that advertisements incorporating humor were more likely to be shared on social media platforms, leading to increased brand exposure and engagement. This underscores the effectiveness of humor in fostering a deeper connection with audiences.

Humor serves as an effective catalyst for holding attention. Infuse your content with tasteful humor and wit, creating moments of levity amidst serious discussions. A well-timed quip or a cleverly inserted anecdote can not only alleviate tension but also foster a warm and inviting atmosphere that keeps readers eagerly anticipating your next line.

Clear and Concise Communication:

Communicate your ideas with clarity and precision. Avoid convoluted sentences and esoteric jargon that might alienate your audience. Strive for simplicity without compromising the depth and nuance of your message. Break down complex concepts into digestible segments, facilitating a seamless flow of information that can be easily grasped and retained.

Consistency and Reliability:

Maintaining a consistent schedule of publication has been instrumental in building trust and reliability. By adhering to a bi-monthly release of my newsletter, I've established a dependable rhythm that my readers have come to anticipate. This consistency has fostered a sense of reliability, assuring my audience that they can rely on me to provide them with enriching content that aligns with their interests and aspirations.

A survey conducted by the Nielsen Norman Group revealed that consistent branding across all platforms can increase revenue by up to 23%. Moreover, a study by MarketingSherpa found that 68% of consumers prefer brands that provide consistent experiences across all channels.

Build trust by consistently delivering high-quality content. Establish a reliable schedule for your publications, maintaining a steady stream of engaging material that keeps your audience actively involved. Demonstrate your commitment to their interests by addressing their feedback, concerns, and suggestions, fostering a symbiotic relationship built on mutual trust and respect.

Call to Action and Further Exploration:

Conclude your content with a compelling call to action that encourages readers to take the next step. Whether it's subscribing to your newsletter, exploring related content, or engaging in a meaningful dialogue, provide clear directives that motivate your audience to continue their journey with you.

In conclusion, my journey as an independent author has taught me that the key to captivating and holding attention lies in understanding my audience, infusing my narratives with relatable experiences, and fostering a dynamic connection built on trust and engagement. By incorporating these personalized strategies, I've not only expanded my readership but also forged meaningful connections that transcend the boundaries of mere readership, fostering a community of individuals united by a shared passion for storytelling and exploration.

The art of captivating and holding attention demands a delicate balance between creativity, empathy, and strategic communication. By employing these multifaceted strategies, you can not only captivate your audience but also foster a lasting connection that transcends mere readership, transforming passive consumers into actively engaged participants in your narrative. Remember, the key lies in understanding your audience, crafting compelling narratives, and fostering a sense of community that encourages continuous interaction and mutual growth.

Understanding audience preferences, incorporating visual content, crafting engaging headlines, integrating humor, fostering interactive engagement, and maintaining consistency are all critical components of successful audience engagement strategies. By aligning one's approach with these findings, authors and content creators can significantly enhance their ability to capture and maintain their audience's attention in an increasingly competitive digital landscape.

<u>Crafting Compelling Speeches and Presentations</u>

I've been giving speeches and presentations for over 20 years, and I've learned a lot about what it takes to craft a compelling message. Whether you're talking to a small group of colleagues or a large audience at a conference, there are a few key things you can do to ensure that your words resonate with your listeners.

Here I'll share some of my best tips for crafting compelling speeches and presentations. I'll also include live examples and instances, as well as recent studies with relevant data on the subject.

Know your audience

The first step to crafting any speech or presentation is to know your audience. Who are you talking to? What do they care about? What do they already know about your topic? Once you understand your audience, you can tailor your message to their specific needs and interests. It is also a lot easier to interact with your audience after you know your audience well.

For example, if you're giving a presentation to a group of potential customers, you'll want to focus on how your product or service can benefit them. If you're giving a speech to a group of students, you'll want to make sure your message is engaging, interactive and relevant to their lives.

A 2020 study by the University of Michigan found that people are more likely to be engaged by a presentation that is interactive. The study found that participants were more likely to pay attention to a presentation and to remember information from it when they were able to participate in the presentation, such as by asking questions or answering polls.

Tell a story

One of the best ways to capture your audience's attention is to tell a story. Stories are relatable and memorable, and they can help to connect with your listeners on an emotional level.

When telling a story, be sure to choose one that is relevant to your topic and that will resonate with your audience. You can also use stories to illustrate your points, to provide humor, or to make your message more memorable.

For example, I once gave a speech to a group of young business trainees about the importance of innovation. I started my speech by telling a story about how I came up with the idea for my book company. The story was relatable and engaging, and it helped to set the stage for my message about the importance of innovation.

A 2021 study by the University of Pennsylvania found that people are more likely to be persuaded by a speaker who uses storytelling. The study found that participants were more likely to agree with the speaker's arguments when the speaker used stories to illustrate their points.

Be passionate

If you're not passionate about your topic, it will show. Your audience will be able to tell if you're not interested in what you're talking about, and they're less likely to be engaged.

That's why it's important to choose a topic that you're passionate about and that you're excited to talk about. If you don't have a passion for your topic, it will be difficult to craft a compelling speech or presentation.

For example, I'm passionate about helping people to communicate more effectively. That's why I love giving speeches and presentations on topics like public speaking and presentation skills. I'm excited to share my knowledge and experience with others, and I can tell that my passion for the topic comes through in my speeches and presentations.

In all of my speeches and presentations, I try to be passionate about my topic. I'm excited to share my knowledge and experience with others, and I can tell that my passion for the topic comes through in my speeches and presentations.

In one speech, I told the story of how I overcame my fear of public speaking. The story was relatable and engaging, and it helped to connect with my audience on an emotional level.

A 2022 study by the University of Minnesota found that people are more likely to be persuaded by a speaker who is passionate about their topic. The study found that participants were more likely to agree with the speaker's arguments when they could see that the speaker was genuinely interested in the topic.

Use visuals

Visuals can be a great way to make your speech or presentation more engaging and informative. They can help to break up your text, add interest, and make your message more memorable.

When choosing visuals, be sure to select ones that are relevant to your topic and that are high quality. Avoid using too much text on your visuals, and make sure they are easy to read and understand.

In another presentation, I used visuals to illustrate my points. I used a series of slides with images and videos to make my presentation more engaging and informative, and to help keep my audience's attention.I also use a whiteboard to write down key ideas and to draw diagrams. The visuals help to make my presentation more engaging and informative, and they help to keep my audience's attention.

A 2023 study by the University of California, Berkeley found that people are more likely to be engaged by a presentation that includes visuals. The study found that participants were more likely to remember information from a presentation when it was accompanied by visuals, such as images, videos, or diagrams.

Practice, practice, practice!

The best way to ensure that your speech or presentation is a success is to practice, practice, practice! Practice in front of a mirror, practice in front of a friend or family member, and even practice in front of an audience if possible.

The more you practice, the more confident you'll be when you deliver your speech or presentation. And when you're confident, your audience will be more likely to be engaged.

Key Takeaways:

- <u>Understanding Your Audience:</u>

Knowing your audience's interests, experiences, and expectations enables you to tailor your story or presentation to their preferences.

Personalizing content to address specific needs and interests fosters deeper audience engagement.

- <u>Compelling Narrative Structure:</u>

Crafting a story or presentation with a clear beginning, middle, and end builds anticipation and sustains audience engagement.

Introducing relatable characters and conflicts creates a more immersive and emotionally resonant narrative.

- <u>Injecting Emotions and Empathy:</u>

Conveying feelings and emotions associated with events fosters a deeper connection with the audience.

Sharing personal experiences and highlighting emotional nuances creates a sense of shared empathy and understanding.

- <u>Descriptive Language and Sensory Details:</u>

Using vivid imagery, evocative language, and sensory descriptions brings settings and experiences to life, enhancing audience immersion.

Describing cultural events and experiences with vibrant details allows the audience to immerse themselves in the narrative.

- <u>Incorporating Suspense and Surprise:</u>

Gradually building suspense and incorporating unexpected twists maintains the audience's curiosity and heightens engagement.

Adding suspense elements to stories and presentations keeps the audience intrigued and captivated.

- <u>Powerful Takeaways:</u>

Conveying valuable lessons or insights ensures a lasting impact on the audience, encouraging reflection and personal growth.

Highlighting the transformative power of resilience and perseverance inspires the audience to approach challenges with a positive mindset.

- <u>Captivating Attention Strategies:</u>

Understanding audience preferences and tailoring content accordingly enhances engagement and resonance.

Employing interactive elements, such as polls and Q&A sessions, fosters a sense of community and active engagement.

- <u>Effective Use of Visuals:</u>

Incorporating relevant images, videos, and diagrams enhances engagement and aids comprehension, making the presentation more memorable.

Utilizing multimedia elements creates a more immersive and visually appealing experience for the audience.

- <u>Crafting Compelling Messages:</u>

Tailoring speeches and presentations to align with audience interests and aspirations increases the likelihood of audience engagement.

Incorporating relatable anecdotes and personal experiences fosters connections and facilitates a deeper understanding of the topic.

- <u>Effective Communication Techniques:</u>

Conveying enthusiasm and passion about the topic resonates with the audience, fostering a deeper connection and engagement.

Ensuring clear and concise communication facilitates easy comprehension and a seamless flow of information.

- <u>Interactive Engagement:</u>

Encouraging active participation and fostering a sense of community through interactive engagement strengthens the bond between the speaker and the audience.

Incorporating humor and wit lightens the atmosphere, creating a more enjoyable and engaging experience for the audience.

- <u>Consistency and Reliability:</u>

Maintaining a consistent publication schedule builds trust and reliability, reassuring the audience of the speaker's commitment to providing valuable content.

Establishing a reliable rhythm of engagement encourages a continuous and interactive relationship with the audience.

- <u>Effective Call to Action:</u>

Concluding presentations with a compelling call to action encourages audience participation and further engagement.

Encouraging readers to subscribe to newsletters, explore related content, or engage in meaningful discussions fosters a continued connection and dialogue.

These key takeaways highlight the essential elements and strategies for mastering the art of storytelling, engaging an audience effectively, and crafting compelling speeches and presentations that resonate with the listeners on an emotional and intellectual level. Understanding the audience, utilizing storytelling techniques, infusing passion and emotion, incorporating visuals, and fostering interactive engagement are all crucial components of creating impactful and memorable content that captivates and holds the audience's attention.

CHAPTER FIVE

SPEAKING FOR SUCCESS - MASTER THE ART AND RHETORIC

FROM STAGE FRIGHT TO STAGE READY

"**B**EING INTROVERTED, DOESN'T MEAN necessarily being shy or being afraid of public speaking; it just means that it' hard for me to interact with people for too long."
-Amy Schumer.

Imagine you see a full-grown giraffe standing in front of your house the moment you step out of your home: a life size, flesh, and blood giraffe. The most immediate question that will come to your mind will be what is giraffe doing in front of my house. Why is the giraffe standing in front of my home? Am I in danger? The human mind wants an immediate answer to these questions.

All other questions about how long it takes to become a full-size giraffe, its natural habitat, etc., take a back seat and can wait. Our brain wants to get to the core area of the central theme or the topic before other unimportant details.

Similarly, the audience first wants to know what will the speaker speak on and why I should listen to him before listening to other details of the speech, dwelling on where, when, how, etc. But talking about what the address is all about and why it is essential to the audience is the two most critical foundations of any speech. In the public speaking lingua, it is called signposting.

Let us take a look at some examples.

"Today, I will talk about my product's quality, affordability, and mass appeal to show why it is a must-buy for your company".

"My 30-minute talk will mainly focus on a sound immune system by eating right".

"We need to emphasize strengthening our company's safety system. And I am going to talk about just that".

In this way, the audience understands the core area of speech or idea and gradually be hooked on to it.

When the audience understand the purpose of the speech, the speaker can then safely proceed to give other details or the message.

So if you accept that the primary role is to ignite the idea into the audience, then here are four practical tips for becoming a good speaker. One. Your speech should primarily revolve around one central idea, and all other reasoning should support that very idea. Hence, reduce your content to that same idea only and give yourself a chance to explain that idea adequately by providing context and sharing examples. Two, give your audience the reason to care. Arouse curiosity among the listeners for your vision. You can use intriguing, provocative questions to underline the listeners' knowledge gap. Once you have sparked that desire, it is much easier to build up the idea in the audience's mind.

Three, build the picture, bit by bit, out of concepts that the audience can easily understand, not in your language but in the language they know. And it is also a good idea to test the talk with your trusted friend to know if there is any part where they get confused. And the fourth tip is, your picture should be worth sharing with the audience at large and not confined to your organization or close circle of friends. The idea should be such that it could brighten up someone's day, or he could see the world from a new perspective, or he could do things differently. If you have that content in your speech, it will indeed be a gift to the audience.

Therefore, the speaker should deliver this message or idea in exact words, depending on the level of understanding that the audience present can easily follow. And remember not to bury the primary information with a plethora of unimportant details while giving a presentation with the help of PowerPoint slides. Use simple language or everyday stories, and examples of terminology which should be easily understood by the audience.

Simplicity is the ultimate sophistication.

Say less, but say it well. That should be the key to an effective presentation. Cut down on anything irrelevant or offensive from your speech. Brevity is the soul of wit. There is no point in talking about everything under the sun. Winston Churchill once said, "A good speech is like a woman's skirt: Long enough to cover the subject and short enough to create interest." Long-winded descriptions lead the speakers to nowhere. The natural substance of your speech should be only dwelling upon what is innovative and novel. That is how the audience will remember your address for a long time and appreciate it as well.

Don't utter anything irrelevant or offensive. Don't try to make others fool by saying anything that may seem funny to you, but has no relevance to what you're supposed to speak. Come up with relevant examples or share your personal experiences. Keep in mind that a good speaker can interest people with his words so that they're bound to listen.

It is well-advised not to lose your individuality while you make a speech. You may be an energetic speaker or flamboyant introvert or extraordinarily extrovert, or even have a combination of different styles. If you stick to your core individuality, if you stick to being yourself, the audience will lap it up and love it. There is room for every style.

When we talk about style, we talk about charisma. You can be charismatic by what you do and how you do and are willing to learn and make extra efforts for it rather than what you are. You can boost your style or charisma by following these ten simple steps.

1.Plan your speech well in advance: Write it down beforehand. Start talking to yourself in a loud voice for two days. Repeat this (I am a strong speaker).

2. Practice the speech in front of a mirror and by heart. Improve your body language and confidence. It could show your level of confidence. Face yourself by the mirror and keep talking with a loud voice for two days—repeat (I am a strong speaker, and I can be whatever I want).

3. Pay attention to body language by keeping your back straight and looking in the eyes of the audience.

4. Making eye contact or looking towards the crowd will indeed show you as a good speaker, even if you have to read out some script or speak from some "learned by heart speech."

5. If possible, walk on the stage while talking. Remember, if you're not confident, the audience will know it before you.

6. Put others' needs above your fears: If you've practised well, surely nothing can go wrong. Take deep

breaths just before the event. Remember, when you're speaking in front of an audience, you're educating them on that topic. So, put their needs above your fear.

7. Do not fear be laughed at; if things do not go as anticipated, then the possibility is that your fear may overwhelm your confidence.

8. There is nothing wrong with accepting that a few knowledgeable people in the audience or something may go wrong somewhere, but it hardly matters. Nonetheless, most genuine people will always support your earnest efforts, and a few people who are not public speakers themselves will doubt you. In such a scenario, you should not care as much as no one bothers.

9. Never underestimate yourself and never overestimate the audience. And remember, there is always next time. On a bad day, learn from your mistake and prepare well for your speech and come out as a winner.

10. Watch recordings of speeches: Watch famous Ted Talks. Watching recordings of some talks of your niche will help you articulate your tone well. Record a video of yourself while talking about random topics every day for two days and observe and improve upon the shortcomings.

Here's a list of ten things that we should consciously avoid while delivering the speech. The results will follow:

1. Do not attempt too many tricks as it can detract you from the point you're trying to get across to your audience.

2. Do not be emotional as it may show you as someone who isn't open to others' points of view.

3. Do not stray from the central theme, as chances are, you may forget from where you started.

4. Do not make up your statistics. There is always a possibility of someone from the audience catching you on the wrong foot.

5. Do not bash individuals or organizations during a speech. You may entertain the audience, but you could never become a good speaker. Do not test the audiences' tolerance levels by dragging on and on with your speech.

6. Do not speak in a monotone or be dominating. Learn to break the monotony. Learn to listen to the audience and answer questions.

7. Never tell your audience that you are boring. It ranks number one on putting yourself down in front of an audience. Do not generalize: Be specific. By generalization, you let people know how ignorant you are of the given topic.

8. Do not make it oblivious to the audience that you are the last-minute replacement for a speaker. Please do not make the audience wonder why they had to sit through that.

9. Do not give clichéd quotes: Come up with something light, new, and yet innovative stories. Do not read from a prepared text on the stage. Instead, remember the key points. Do not tell about your personal life as it interests no one but you. Keep the family stories out of the speech unless relevant to the given topic.

10.Similarly, your achievements are significant to no one but you. Refrain from highlighting yourself. Be modest. Do not give just a regular speech and nothing remarkable which would make people forget it immediately. A typical address would mean you've failed to create an impact on the audience. Do not fail to get quality feedback from someone you think will review your content and suggest changes. Never give "It's not my day" excuse for a poor speech. Everyone has a bad day.

Learning from your mistakes and evolving decides how good a speaker you are.

A) Role of speaker is similar to orchestra instructor or conductor.

i)The role of a good speaker is somewhat akin to that of the orchestra instructor or a conductor who is a "frontman" of sorts. Just as it is essential to have a competent conductor for a rocking performance, an expert speaker will leave his audience spellbound with his mesmerizing description and details. A lot of confidence in himself, good content, and the ability to freely express are three primary ingredients to make you a successful speaker. Hence know how and when to modulate your voice. That is the most critical thing while speaking; you must know when to be soft, stern, and pleasant. Just like the orchestra conductor who knows when and how to indicate for the next set of music notes

ii)A genuine smile while you speak, has a charmingly soothing effect. Your tone matters more than your accent does; looking directly into the audience while you say, making a few eye contacts, and not shying away has a profound effect.

iii)An honest smile on your face will add confidence to your stature while addressing the gathering; it also psychologically urges people to feel the honesty in your delivery. Look around because you make them feel involved in your words as you look at them. You also let your eyes do the talking as well.

iv)But how do you develop these skills? By practising well before the mirror. And also, before your well-meaning friends. Look at the video recordings of your practice sessions and learn from the mistakes.

v) The subject matter or the topic you will speak should be the next thing in your mind.

A well-informed person who knows what he is about to speak can naturally deliver better.

On the other hand, people who know nothing about the subject matter but can speak well, charmingly and convincingly, though having an excellent quality are not considered good speakers. Giving misinformation is not a trait of a good speaker, however eloquent he may be. But to be well informed and not able to express isn't a good quality of a speaker either.

Hence when a good speaker continues to work on his three core areas, i.e., confidence, charm, and knowledge, he will develop himself to become a good speaker.

vi)The most significant impediment that comes your way is the fear of facing an audience, and this fear is quite common. If you want to become an efficient public speaker first, you need to say 'goodbye fear.'

To build up confidence and fight stage fright, as soon as you reach the stage and face the audience, you should imagine yourself as a rock star and one of the most outstanding speakers whom the audience is eagerly waiting to hear. Say to yourself; I am the best. Have ample confidence in yourself. You stand before the audience because they expect something from you when speaking to them. Your enthusiasm to talk to the people you address reflects the leadership qualities you may have to persuade them to see your point of view.

vii)**Remember content is the king.** Try to develop good content of what you are going to speak. Try to read as many different books as you can on the subject matter, which can help immensely. Try reading books, novels, magazines, newspapers, articles, etc. Though you may not remember everything you read, reading adds substantially to your knowledge, and you have sufficient knowledge about what you are speaking so that you can firmly stay with yourself.

While doing this, save new words and phrases that you come across and build up your vocabulary. It would help if you had words to express yourself. It would help if you even had more words to understand what the other speaker said. The excellent combination of reading and speaking will ensure that over the time, you become a good speaker. Besides speaking skills, the content will connect you with the audience. If it is compelling and unique, people will admire you for it.

viii)Besides, instead of speaking for hours on generally known things, share your unique personal experiences too. Good speakers arouse interest in the audience's mind with their words. Besides, the audience loves it when you are your humorous best, which will keep your audience engaged. However, refrain from saying something you may find funny, but is out of context and has no relevance to what you are supposed to speak. Stand-up comedians or humorous celebrities are perhaps better public speakers. They ensure that whatever they have to convey reaches their audience directly, effectively, and unadulterated.

ix)One of the significant factors for their efficacy is their honesty. They speak their minds without bothering much, and their verbal "onslaught" is timely too. They observe things around them quite minutely, while writing their script, laced with humour and wit as a bonus give away. They become popular with the people due to this very reason.

x) For more than one hour a day, just about every day, search your language libraries for content that interests you and download them. It would help if you studied on the go wherever you are and whenever you have the time after transferring them to your phone or MP3 player. You will start with short, more accessible content and graduate to longer, more exciting content. Just keep doing it. Ideally, listen to the material with the transcript to have a better chance of understanding it.

To be an efficient public speaker, you have to practice constantly. Be regular and practice at regular intervals. The more you will practice, the better you will become each time. To begin with, start speaking in front of a small select audience like your friends, then a small group of a like-minded bunch of people and to practice systematically, take part in local or friendly competitions, you can join any public speakers club too. Do whatever is possible and bring out the best in you.

B) **Imitate and speak**

While you are listening to the podcast or a recorded speech on U Tube, imitating out loud the odd word or phrase that you may come across is a good idea too. It is commonly referred to as shadowing. But you may need even more practice at getting the words out. You may attentively listen for a few minutes to the content for which you have the transcript, where you like the voice, and how the person speaks. After listening, read the exact text aloud and imitate how the person says.

Focus on the rhythm and intonation. Don't worry about the words you mispronounce; get the rhythm and flow. Do this over and over. Get your voice modulation correct. See if it matches with the speaker on the podcast.

It will be even better to find someone you can speak to. Online sites, such as Ling Q, where you can find native speakers to talk with is of help too. Mispronounced words should not be a cause for worry while we speak. By sending the conversation report with a list of words and phrases that caused trouble, sent by Online sites such as Ling Q invariably help the learners.

This report comes in handy in improving our pronunciation in subsequent practice sessions. What is essential is to get over the fear psychosis of speaking and speaking more often on topics of mutual interest.

C) **Write**

Writing helps us express ourselves even better without the pressure of speaking with someone. You may not feel like writing much at first. The Ling Q dictation function is another way to get into writing. You can even submit your report to Ling Q for subsequent corrections, if any.

Public speakers acquire a particular speaking skill set over a while. To excel as an efficient public speaker, you must master the techniques like voice modulation, control over hand gestures, and stage usage. You will see a significant shift in your general speaking abilities as soon as you master these techniques.

D) **Record your voice**

To get the pronunciation right, we can record our voice now and then listen to the audio and compare it with the native speaker. Listen to the original speaker and then register your voice having the same transcript and compare the two and work on the difference, if any. Try to notice the subtle difference in pronunciation. By seeing the difference, you will have a better chance to improve your pronunciation.

Key Take Away

1. Primarily revolve around one central idea when preparing the text for the speech

2. Arouse curiosity among the listeners so that their minds may allow your idea to be seeded

3. Build the idea, bit by bit, out of concepts that the audience can easily understand

4. Idea should be worth sharing with the audience

5. Say less but say it well

6. Don't utter anything irrelevant or offensive

7. Stick to your core individuality

8. Be charismatic by following these ten simple steps

a) Plan your speech well in advance

b) Practice the speech in front of a mirror

c) Pay attention to body language

d) Making eye contact

e) If possible, walk on the stage while talking

f) Put others' needs above your fears

g) Do not fear being laughed at

h) There is nothing wrong to accept that there may be a few knowledgeable people in the audience

i) Never underestimate yourself and never overestimate the audience

j) Watch recordings of speeches

9. Ten things to be avoided.

a) Do not attempt too many tricks as it can detract you

b)Do not be emotional

c)Do not stray from the central theme,

d)Do not make up your statistics.

e)Do not bash individuals or organizations during a speech

f)Do not speak in a monotone or be dominating.

g)Never tell your audience that you are boring.

h)Do not make it oblivious to the audience that you are a last-minute replacement as a speaker.

i)Do not give clichéd quotes

j)Refrain from highlighting yourself.

10. Role of speaker is similar to orchestra instructor or conductor

11. A genuine smile, while you speak has a charmingly soothing effect

12. Your tone matters more than your accent does

13. Practicing well first before the mirror and then before your well-meaning friends and also by looking at the video recordings of your practice sessions

14. The three core areas of good oratory are confidence, charm, and knowledge

15. Content is the king. Try to develop good content of what you are going to speak. Try to read as many different genres of books

16. Save new words and phrases that you come across and build up your vocabulary

17. Be humorous best, and this will keep your audience engaged

18. Search language libraries for content that interests you and download them, listen to material where you also have the transcript

19. To begin with, start speaking in front of a small select audience like your friends

20. After listening, read the exact text aloud and imitate how the person speaks.

21. Online sites such as Ling Q help the learners

22. Writing helps in expressing ourselves even better

23. Master the techniques like voice modulation, control over hand gestures, and stage usage

24. Try recording your voice, listen to the audio, and then compare it with the native speaker

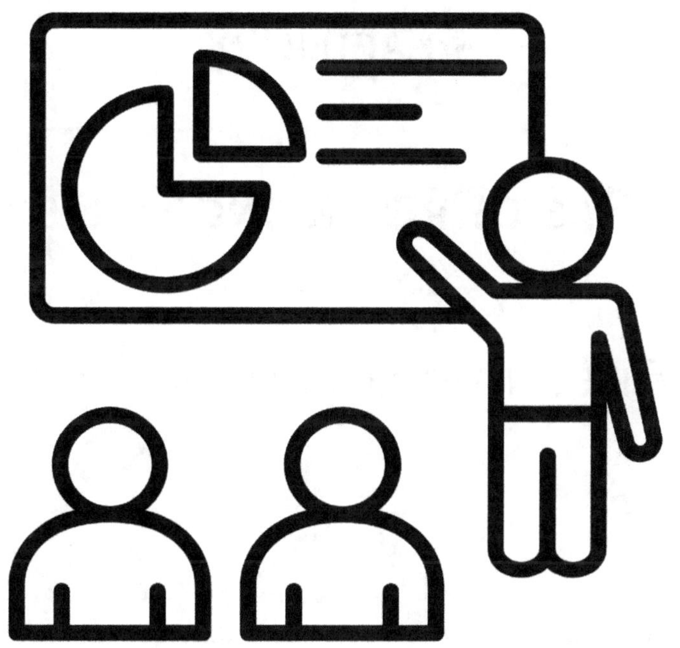

Chapter Six

Basic Presenting Skills

Direct to Mind Communication

"WHEN SPEAKING IN PUBLIC, your message—no matter how important—will not be effective or memorable if you don't have a clear structure."
-Patricia Fripp.

History is replete with illustrious examples of how some of the legendary orators have carved out a niche for themselves. It is for us to find out the approach they adopted to attain the pinnacle of success they achieved in good oratory. Let us find out the basic tenets that encompass to form the firm foundation and strong structure of a great presenting.

First and foremost, any impressive presenting and public oratory begins with an impactful, pertinent and unforgettable introduction; it could be in the form of a :-

- narrative
- information
- declaration
- query
- statistic
- or something more appealing

If, at the very beginning, the presenter can garner the listeners' interest by interrupting their thought process, half the battle is already won. You as a presenter should be able to say, do or show something which sets you apart from other fellow speakers, which would, in turn, ignite the thought, interest, and curiosity of the listeners.

1. Bond with your viewers

The core of any good presenting is the actual bonding with your viewers. You can bond with them by showing that you are part of them and have some commonality by building their confidence. The connection begins when they start to see that the orator is one among them who have shared knowledge, challenge, and ambition.

The moment the orator can make his listener understand the course they are now and where they desire to be, the gates of an excellent presentation open up. People trust people who understand and are similar to them. Appreciation of each other develops, leading to trust when two similar thinking people interact.

2. Believe in your message

Great orators are great believers in their message. The process starts by first and foremost understanding your viewers well before your presentation day. How fresh and relevant your content of the speech may be, it is your personal belief that what you are going to tell your listeners will change their outlook towards life, which is a crucial factor of a great presenting.

You should be so thorough with your topic that all questions from the audience should be answered. A systematic practice would also ensure that your talk is appealing and impactful. All great orators positively help listeners in making their lives happier and better.

3. **Use of the three things**

Generally, people like things in 3's; divide your script into three parts. Share three essential elements, or give your audience three ways to work on your presentation.

Thoughts or ideas presented in threes are intrinsically more prone to generate curiosity.

4. **Play with your voice**

All great orators are good voice artists. They can attract their listeners by lowering the pitch of their voice for dramatic effect or can raise their voice to underline their point of view. Similarly, the orators change the rhythm and pace to have the desired impact on the audience. In other words, they carry their well-organized orchestra with them to effectively convey their message with a more significant effect.

Here are some examples of playing your orchestra effectively.

- Emphasize a word, an important statement of fact, and practice pausing

- Increase the speed of your delivery for building up the thrill.

You can say things at a slow pace. It may also sound authoritative.

5. **Keep it simple**

Great talks are simple talks. So simple that even an eight-year-old can understand it. It should be free from all technical jargon and high-sounding vocab. The message should be short, focused, and to the point. Do not give an overdose of data and information. Come quickly to the end, and this is what exactly you want them to remember. Simplicity in your talk will lead to easy understanding and acceptance of the idea by the listeners. Surveys have shown that the listeners generally switch off their minds when they have to work extra hard to understand what is being told.

6. **Do not present but converse**

All good orators tend to come on a conversational mode rather than a presentation mode when giving speeches. The listeners are interested in your stories. They are interested in relating your personal experiences and in enjoying your sense of humour. The audience should feel as if they are sitting in their living room and having a lively discussion.

7. **Using PowerPoint**

The use of PowerPoint and slides helps the viewers remember the message for a longer duration. Hence, pictures, colour contrast can be imaginatively used in PowerPoint presentations. Skilfully crafted visuals accompanied with very few words have the power to impact the viewers' minds. The presenter should not read what is written on the slide. PowerPoint can work if you breathe life into it.

8. **Making a difference**

The listener gives his attention to the orator as he has something important to say that may bring value to his life and help bring about a positive difference. All great orators are well aware of this. If their speeches make a difference in the viewers' lives, they are long remembered for it.

9. **Connect with listeners emotionally**

To make the proper connection with the listeners, the orator has to create the right atmosphere. To do this, he has to know the mood of his listeners and respond to it accordingly. Any enlightened orator would ponder what my viewer needs to learn instead of what I need to present?

10. **Start, end strongly.**

Good presenters have both their start and end of presentation equally solid and dramatic. Instead of the final slide showing thank you or questions, they close with a powerful quote, fact, story, or a statement, or a thought-provoking question, a challenge or a request, or something even more dramatic.

We have to ensure that the end of a talk is as powerful as its beginning. We have to find out what best works for us as an orator.

Key Take Away

Say something at the beginning that would attract the listeners' attention.
1)Have full conviction in your message
Have a strong belief that whatever message you are going to convey to the audience will impact them in a better way
2)Thoughts or ideas presented in threes are intrinsically more prone to generate curiosity.
3)Play with your voice

Voice modulation while giving a speech gives a better impact on the listeners

4)Keep it simple

Simple the presentation, longer the listeners, are going to retain it

5)Do not present but converse

The listeners should feel that they are discussing an issue while sitting in their drawing-room. Hence, whatever is told should be in conversational mode and not in the presentational form

6)While using PowerPoint

The PowerPoint slides may have pictures and colours with minimum words.

7)Making a difference

Your speech should make a positive impact on the lives of the audience

8)Connect with listeners emotionally

Give your speech what your listeners need to know instead of thinking about what you need to present

9)Start, end strongly.

Both starting and ending of the talk should be on an impactful note.

TAKE A BREAK

We have reached a midpoint of the book. You may like to take a break and give feedback on this book in the form of a rating or a review on Amazon or Goodreads . This will help immensely in spreading the message in the reading community.

Besides, your suggestions are incredibly important to my creative process as an independent writer. It not only fuels my passion but also allows me to go deeply into the core of my creative attempts and find the very heart of my writing. I respectfully ask that you think about posting a review/rating for "The Eloquent Mindset" in order to gain your useful insights and opinions.

It is not necessary for your review to be in-depth or extensive; even a brief collection of ideas that expresses your true feelings will do. Whether your comments are compliments or constructive criticism, they all serve as important building bricks in my search for ongoing development as a writer and storyteller.

You might prefer to scan the QR code below using your smartphone.

Scan this image with your smart phone and leave a review or a rating on Amazon

Chapter Seven

Unlocking the Most Engaging, Charismatic Self for Public Speaking

---

Social Neuroscience in Public Speaking and Presentations

"**T**HE RIGHT WORD MAY be effective, but no word was ever as effective as a rightly timed pause."
– *Mark Twain.*

1) A lot happens in our brain

When we hear an inspirational and powerful speaker, a lot happens in our brains. Besides, when we speak before an audience, we too can cause a positive neurological reaction in others' brains. We can achieve this by telling simple stories woven around our facts and information in our presentation.

Our brains are hard-wired for levels. We have been telling stories around camp fires since our cavemen and women days. When we describe a story, our audience's mind releases Dopamine. Dopamine is the hormone that is responsible for memory. So it acts as a mental sticky note. When we tell an audience a story, we let them release the hormone, which makes them remember the account for a longer duration.

There is a recent study on memory retention. It says if we hear, we remember something; if we see something, we place a little more, if we both see and hear something, we remember even more, but if we experience emotions that stimulate our brains, we remember almost 80% of it. Stories can do this because of the dopamine release. So next time you want your audience to remember your presentation, wrap it around a story as it is data with a soul.

We mostly remember the First and Last things told to us. Most of the time, we recall the first and the last experience more than anything else. Our brains work that way only. However, we like that our audience should remember our entire presentation. Hence, we have to introduce in our presentation a story and end it with a "soul" that typically sticks and helps the listener recall it.

2) Audience Engagement

Engaging the audience is an essential element of any presentation. The more we engage our audience during the presentation, the more we tend to make it accepted and receivable by the audience. There was a great experiment to show that if there is no audience engagement, the heartbeat level goes down, as shown in the electrocardiogram machines attached to the section of the listeners. The heartbeat level went down at the end of every ten minutes.

We are hard-wired to retain information when we are doing something or moving and not when we are sitting still. Hence it is essential to keep the audience engaged if we do not want our audience to tune out or their heartbeat rate to nose dive. We must interact with the audience at least every 10 minutes of the offline presentation and every 4 minutes of the online or virtual presentation. Give a video quote or throw up a question or have a group discussion or activity, anything that can shake out the audience from the lull that may have gripped the audience from the straight lecturing.

3) **Practice- Neutralizing the threat reaction**

We now move from audience engagement to another essential element of public speaking, i.e., brain practice. Neurons that fire together wire together. It means that we are building neurons superhighways in our brains every time we practise. e.g., If we are driving with the help of Google maps and it's taking us through unknown turns and sites, we tend to get even more stressed because we are not familiar with the route taken.

On the other hand, if we take well-known routes which we take every day, and are familiar with the surroundings, buildings, and signage, we are pretty confident in reaching our destination without any stress. It is the same in the case of public speaking. If we are familiar with the script's presentation well, we are sure of the delivery. We are, in other words, building neurons superhighways where we are pretty confident in travelling safely. Our brains crave safety. Our brains reject unsafe conditions and readily accept safe ones.

A well-practised presentation with a bigger neuron superhighway is a safe condition for our brain to accept. Right from our caveman days, our brains like to work in safe conditions, in those environments where we are familiar and have performed repeatedly.

Because in such a scenario where our brains feel it is entering into unchartered or unfamiliar territory or a new habitat, it shuts down immediately. Our brain shuts down or goes into a threat reaction mode in several ways. It can procrastinate. It can find reasons not to practice as it is very overwhelming and threatening. You have bitten off too much. You take baby steps to complete the practice's in such a scenario.

4) Negativity Bias

While talking about the threat reaction is vital, starting from our early caveman and cavewoman days, we are hard-wired to remember all adverse events and episodes in our lives for a more extended period. e.g., rustling in the bushes was taken as a tiger lurking behind the bushes, a dangerous situation and would clear off from the area—the caveman associated this negative occurrence in his mind for a more extended period. From our early planet days, we are hard-wired to remember negativity or negative circumstances for a more extended period. Adverse events or occurrences hang on to our minds like sticky tape or Velcro.

At the same time, positive events or circumstances are like a Teflon, where we do not hang on to that. However, the negative bias that we experience is almost ten times more powerful than the positive thoughts as we are hard-wired or programmed in such a way right from our early cave inhabiting days. Hence, if we do not allow ourselves to fail, we keep thinking about one damaging episode that occurred during our presentation, and if we do not let ourselves take a baby step one at a time, we cannot proceed forward.

5) Permit to fail forward

We must permit ourselves to fail forward with grace, make mistakes, and take baby steps. When you hear these negative voices within you, it is an ancient reaction called negative bias, which is your brain's way of consciously protecting you from the unchartered territory.

These are, but with a difference. These are full of potholes, pits, and dangers. We should not hang on to these negative thoughts and, on the other hand, should rewire our brains to some positive reviews. Instead of thinking about how I will give this dreadful presentation, one can ponder and say, oh, I will contribute something that matters to the group.

I am looking forward to teaching and sharing my perspective through this presentation. We are building new neural pathways that will rewire our brains to achieve this.

6) **Overcome Fear**

Our brains are dumb because, in two million years, it has hardly distinguished between 'Fear' of giving a speech and 'Fear' of being ambushed by a tiger. It knows just 'Fear', and whenever it senses a threat perception, whether it is about being attacked by a tiger or a threat of a doomed presentation, our brain signal's the fight or flight mechanism to release itself. It is essential to know that 'Fear' of public speaking is a full-bodied automatic hormonal response to what our brain considers to be a threat.

Once our body goes into fight or flight mode, it often derails our presentation. We often feel guilty and blame ourselves when nervous before making a public speech.

7) **Be kind to yourselves**

A peep into its neuroscience will help us be a little kinder to ourselves as it is just a well-meaning friend who is jacked up on red bull and giving a bad advice. It is trying to protect you from something that is not a threat. After all, giving a presentation is not going to kill you. But our brains think it might so, hence it is in a protective mode.

8) Tackle fight or flight mechanism

The brain does not need to release the fight or flight mechanism. It is essential to be able to talk to this fear. It is necessary to speak to this well-meaning friend and say, "hey, Fear, I see the threat running away; thank you for saving me from getting lost in the dark jungle or the wilderness. Today I am just giving a presentation to sit back and relax. While preparing for the presentation, take a long breath and calm down.

The neuroscience behind breath works because it is fascinating to become an alchemist to your body chemistry when you learn to incorporate your diaphragm. You can take your body out of fight or flight mode and switch it to rest and digest.

9) Take a long breath at pauses

By knowing how to breathe, you can change your brain chemistry for the better to give powerful and confident presentations. And you don't feel like Fear which is a tidal wave that takes you over, and you're powerless until it washes away. You can become your chemist to your brain chemistry.

10) **Smile and make eye contact**

While making a presentation, when you smile and make eye contact with the audience, it is said that their brains release hormones (serotonin dopamine). It is the same bonding hormone that mothers and babies release when they nurse.

The studies further show that you connect with your audience authentically by clicking from your eyes and smiling. You help them make sure that they resonate with your message while having a good experience in your presentation.

Besides, a mirror neurons effect is taking place, which is so familiar with babies and their parents. We as babies mirror the behaviour of our mothers and fathers. If they smile, we smile; if they are upset, we feel upset too.

Similarly, when parents make faces, babies mirror them. Our audience is no different. If the audience sees the presenter speaking with joy and passion, they will, and if the presenter is easy going or full of anxiety, the audience will be too.

Key Take Away

1) **A lot happens in our brain**

a)When we speak before an audience, we too can cause a positive neurological reaction in others' brains.

b)When we tell a story, our audience's mind releases Dopamine

c)Dopamine is the hormone that is responsible for memory.

d)If we have some emotions that stimulate our brains, we remember almost 80% of it

e)Stories can stimulate emotions which in turn releases Dopamine.

f)We mostly remember the First and Last things told to us

2)**Audience Engagement**

a)The more we engage our audience during the presentation, the more we tend to make it accepted and receivable by the audience

3)Practice - Neutralizing the threat reaction

a)It means that every time we practise, we build neurons superhighways in our brains.

b)Neurons that fire together wire together.

c)Practice well and be quite sure of the delivery.

4)Negativity Bias

a)We are hard-wired to remember all adverse events and episodes in our lives for a more extended period

b)The negative bias that we experience is almost ten times more powerful than the positive thoughts

5)Permit to fail forward

a)permit ourselves to fail forward with grace and to make mistakes, and take baby steps

7) Be kind to yourself

6) Overcome Fear

8)Tackle flight and fight mechanism

9) **Take a long breath at pauses**

10)**Smile and make eye contact**

CHAPTER EIGHT

TEN USEFUL WAYS OF TALKING TO ANYBODY

HOW TO TALK AND HOW TO LISTEN.

"THERE ARE CERTAIN THINGS in which mediocrity is not to be endured, such as poetry, music, painting, public speaking."
-Jean de la Bruyere.

Have we lost the balance between listening and speaking? How does one talk to just anyone? While talking about the weather and your health (not necessarily in that order) may not be the safest way to start a conversation.

Topics as safe as these may sometimes lead to controversies, especially in the context of climate change and medical ethics. Issues such as politics, religion, child care, food, etc., are best avoided for starting a conversation.

A recent study has shown we stand more polarized and divided today than ever before. We are increasingly losing the habit of listening to each other. We are not likely to compromise the critical decisions that affect our lives based on what we perceive proper.

The right mix of conversation needs a good balance of talking and listening. We are losing that balance as we increasingly adopt the modern means of communication in the digital era.

As we increasingly rely on our smart phones and other intelligent digital gadgets, we lose our ability to acquire interpersonal skills. We are texting with our friends and well-wishers rather than talking or listening to them on one-on-one basis.

A recent study showed that when school kids were asked to speak on a subject of their choice without making notes, a majority found it a daunting and overwhelming task. It is because though we spend hours looking at our computer or mobile screen, we are not talking or listening to our friends and peers face to face and thereby losing our ability to have a continued, consistent and positive conversation.

Suppose you know how to interview people; you would, in turn, also learn how to be a better conversationalist. When we have great conversations, chances are we come out inspired, happier, engaged, understood, connected, etc. And there is no reason whatsoever that our everyday interactions cannot be like that.

10 Basic rules to have a great conversation.

1. Pay attention

When having a conversation, do not multi-task. Be in the moment when you are having a conversation. Do not start thinking about the issues you are facing in the office or about the presentations you are required to make for tomorrow's meeting or what you will have for lunch. When you want to get out of the conversation, get out of it entirely and not half in and half out of it.

2. Do not sermonize

Everyone is an expert in something. Authentic listening requires setting aside your personal opinion. Enter every conversation, assuming that you have something new to learn.

When the speaker senses this acceptance, he is likely to be less vulnerable and is expected to open up the inner niche of his mind to the listener.

3. Use open-ended questions

Just like they teach you in any journalism school, be curious and use open-ended questions for a good conversation and start your question with 5 Ws and 1 H, i.e., who, what, when, where, why, or how.

Hence, try asking a question where your listener is required to think, and the answer would then be much more elaborately interesting. Such as, How did you feel at that moment? If you put in a complicated question, you're going to get a simple answer out. If I ask you, "Were you terrified?" you're going to respond to the most powerful word in that sentence, which is "terrified," and the answer is "Yes, I was" or "No, I wasn't." "Were you angry?" "Yes, I was furious." Let them describe it.

They're the ones that know. Try asking them things like, "What was that like?" "How did that feel?" What challenges have you faced while studying at this University ?" Because then they might have to stop for a moment and think about it, and you're going to get a much more interesting response. Research has shown that people who ask questions are liked by their partners than people who ask fewer questions or keep mum.

4. **Go with the flow- go off script**

Let the thoughts that invade your minds come with a flow and allow them to go out of your mind after they have served their purpose. Let the stories and ideas come and go. You may skip the stock question (Where do you live. What do you do etc.). Be genuine when asking a question, making a statement, or answering. Because people want to know who you are before they reveal themselves.

Often we hear interviews where the guest goes on for a few minutes and the interviewer, lost in his thoughts about his next question, asks a question that the guest has already answered. What happens when the interviewer has stopped listening two minutes back and is ready to shoot a pre-decided question without hearing the guest who has already responded to the question in his deliberation.

Skip the stock questions and start with a statement: "This painting confuses me" or "I can't believe how crowded the train is today." Statements are invitations

116

for the listener to contribute to the conversation., And whether you're asking a question, replying, or making a statement, be authentic. Before people can express themselves, they would like to know you as a person.

5. Be frank and say: "I do not know" when you do not know

When you know the subject well, give your opinion. Keep mum or say you do not see the issue well when ignorant about it. Never attempt to provide false or information based on hearsay. Say that you don't know when you do not know.

6. Don't equate your experience with theirs.

It is never good to start talking about your office when somebody talks about his work environment. Every individual is different, and his experience towards his life will be other than yours. It is never the same. No two individual experiences are similar. Moreover, it's not about you. It is about that individual who is talking. It is best to respect his individuality and hear his experience.

7. Give compliments and try not to repeat yourself.

Giving compliments puts the listener mentally at ease and makes him feel good. It, in turn, helps to get past the initial awkward moments.

Besides, while in conversation, repeating oneself gets dull and pompous.

We do not have to repeat or rephrase ourselves when talking with office colleagues or kids. We do not have to do that.

8. Have more conversations with people you don't know and stay out of the unwanted details

When we meet unknown people, we fear talking to them and fear social rejection. Research has revealed that people are ever eager to speak whenever prompted by someone.

During conversations, there are certain things that people do not care about, such as names, dates, years, and other details for which our minds have to struggle a lot, remembering them. People care more about you what they have in common with you. Hence, it's best to forget about the unwanted details.

9. Be the first to initiate the talk and listen

Despite the awkwardness in talking to people utterly unknown to us, despite the unsure foothold and gaffe, talking is good for us as we are social beings. Minimal chatting tends to boost our mood. In a recent study, the participants were asked to chat with strangers. They were required to note their feelings before and after the interaction.

Although the participants felt their companions were far more interesting before the exchange started, almost all of them said their conversations went way beyond their expectations.

Once having initiated the discussion, it is essential to listen to your companion. You are not listening when you are speaking. Hence when we are silent, we should be listening instead of our mind wandering elsewhere. It is perhaps one of the most critical elements when we are in conversation. We usually prefer to speak. Because if we talk, we are in command; we do not have to hear anything we are not interested in. It takes power and effort to listen to someone.

But if we are not listening, we are simply two people shouting out two differently related sentences at the same time and place. We have to listen to one another. Stephen Covey said it very wonderfully. He said, "Most of us don't listen with the intent to understand. We listen with the intent to reply." We need to listen actively without just nodding our heads.

10: **Talk about something in common and be short**

You can always find out something shared between you and the listener.

It could be birth or work, a familiar friend, a shared hobby, or typical roles or studies. There is no point in overestimating the difference from one another. In actuality, there are many commonalities; all we have to do is go deeper and dig it out.

A good conversation is like a miniskirt; short enough to retain interest, but long enough to cover the subject.

To conclude:

Be interested in other people.

Keep your mouth shut as often as possible, but keep your mind open, and be prepared to be amazed, and you will never be disappointed.

Hence go out, talk to people, listen to people, and, most importantly, be prepared to be amazed.

Key Take Away

1.Learn the balance between speaking and listening.

2.Topics as safe as weather and health may also lead to controversies.

3.We are increasingly losing the habit of listening to each other.

4.We are losing our ability to acquire interpersonal skills.

5.Know the art of interviewing people.

6.10 Basic rules to have a great conversation.

7.Pay attention

8.Do not sermonize.

9.Use open-ended questions

10.Go with the flow- go off script

11.Be frank and say: "I do not know" when you do not know

12.Don't equate your experience with theirs.

13.Give compliments and try not to repeat yourself

14.Have more conversations with people you don't know and stay out of the unwanted details

15.Be the first to initiate the Talk and Listen

16.Talk about something in common and be short

CHAPTER NINE

BUILDING UP A QUICK RAPPORT

HOW TO BREAK THE ICE

"**F**EAR PARALYSES YOU - fear of flying, fear of the future, fear of leaving a rubbish marriage, fear of public speaking, or whatever it is." *-Annie Lennox.*

How often we shudder at the thought of speaking to strangers. The very idea of seeing and meeting an unknown person becomes a big challenge for us. It is normal to feel nervous and awkward when meeting new people.

124

However, if we keep in mind a few simple steps, even talking to an unfamiliar person would be an occasion to look forward to with enthusiasm.

1. **Dress up nicely**

One of the easiest ways to get noticed is dressing up well for the occasion. When you dress up for the event, be it a business meeting, a family gathering, a social event, or just attending the Parent-Teacher Meeting (PTM) of your kid's school, you are already making a statement through our attire even without speaking a word. Our clothing need not be too expensive. But it should attract attention and give the feeling that you have taken care to be dressed up for the occasion.

Whatever one wears should be relevant to the event. It is a good idea to have something such as a tie pin or ring or shoes or watch, which may ignite interest and start a conversation, especially in a networking gathering. It is not necessary to go for anything expensive. However, it will serve the purpose so long as it can arouse interest in others' minds.

2. Starting the conversation, "Breaking the Ice."

One of the most challenging parts is opening the conversation with an unfamiliar person or a group of persons. People generally wonder how to start the discussion. In such a situation, the easiest thing to do is to introduce yourself and initiate the conversation, or, taking a cue from an ongoing debate, you can maneuver it towards an episode or an incident that would reflect your credibility.

3. Boast without boasting

Another way to get noticed with unfamiliar people is when you can relate an incident from your past and compare it with your present position, which would show how much hard work you put in to achieve it. In that case, the focus would not be about your current situation but about the actual struggle you undertook to achieve the present status.

4. Be the storyteller

A good storyteller always becomes the centre of attraction in any social gathering. However, one must practice what one says in facing friends and well-wishers before becoming an apt storyteller. While talking in social groups invariably, successful people have one or two incredible stories up their sleeves, which relate much to the pleasures and appreciation of the people listening to them.

But to reach up to that level of proficiency in storytelling, one must continue to practice without giving in—Marvel people with your stories woven around your ideas, vision, and accomplishments.

5. First is the last impression

When meeting someone for the first time, we invariably try to present our best in terms of how we appear and our delivery content. It is, after all, a big deal. But here is a catch. You will be accepted if you expect it. The optimistic feeling emanating from you will most likely help you gain confidence and ensure your acceptance.

But on the other hand, you are most likely to feel unwanted and redundant if you wish to be rejected and defensive feelings overwhelm you. To conclude, it is best to present yourself as a smiling, confident, and self-assured person who would make the most delicate first impression for any meeting or event.

It is always better to think about a few opening lines. Rehearse them thoroughly before the meeting. Practice it aloud while repeating the lines slowly but clearly. When the person you have addressed hears these lines, they will help build a positive impression about you in his mind.

6. Open yourself up.

When you are meeting someone for the first time, instead of trying to drop names and trying to impress yourself, open yourself up honestly as best as you can. Research shows that when two people genuinely open their hearts out and share their inner feelings and understand each other's vulnerability, the relationship between them stays on a more extended basis.

As both the conversationalists open up to reveal their core strengths and weaknesses, the association will flourish for a longer duration.

7. **Encourage another person to talk about themselves**

People wonder what do they talk about in their first meeting. Instead, one should ask oneself how to make the other person talk about himself. The most pleasurable thing for a person to say is to talk about himself. People like to talk about themselves. "Self-disclosure is extra rewarding," said Harvard neuroscientist Diana Tamir. "People are even willing to forgo their money to talk about themselves," Ms. Timir said.

While you get him to open up during your first meeting, it is best to hear him with an open mind. It's always good to hear somebody without being critical about him and getting to know his aspirations, desires, hopes, and dreams. At the same time, you have to restrain the urge to speak about yourself unless you are specifically asked about it.

People who do not rush into talking about themselves and remain fully tuned to what is being said are considered the best conversationalists. They are the most sought after in times of family crisis, where someone is needed to listen to the issues at hand without being judgemental. You may repeat two or three words that were last spoken or paraphrase, or you can just sum up in your own words what was just said. By doing this, you become an active listener.

8. **Similarity breeds likeability**

Research has shown that we are likely to prefer those people or things that have something in common with us. It could be our name, way of dressing, place of birth, even liked color, etc. We are most likely to get attracted to someone more similar to us than someone opposite us. If we complement each other, we are more likely to stay longer as friends.

9. **Travel, Compliments, and Advice**

The expert thinks that one of the most favored topics for initiating quick responses, even on first meetings, is starting a travel talk. Compliments work almost every time, even if they are somewhat bordering on flattery. Seeking advice from someone is another sure-shot way of creating a conversation. It is a win-win situation for both. While you gain from the valued advice given by an expert, he, on the other hand, feels elevated as an expert on the subject.

10. **Stir up passion.**

What is the best way to start a conversation? If we speak with feelings and emotions, we draw greater attention and arouse interest. A message without emotions and enthusiasm is bland information that is not absorbed by the listener and without any desired effect. When we speak with emotion, the listener is filled with anxiety or anticipation.

The speaker can build up the listener's anxiety or anticipation level to his advantage. The listener is thus swayed easily by the speaker by his speech.

A deft speaker can leverage this to his advantage in any presentation or while making a formal speech. The talk goes to a higher level by using emotionally charged words such as "I am missing you." It is when words are spoken with greater feelings.

The climax of such conversation can be reached while using innermost feelings to express oneself. It has to be used with much discretion after ascertaining how the listener will react. "I keep introspecting about you, and I am afraid of losing you."

Finally, one should also know how to close the conversation. A few phrases that help us in ending the meeting, such as "Finally," "Lastly," or "Giving regards," or phrases like "It was nice speaking to you." In the end, the person you have spoken to should walk away a much more delighted and happier person. That is how we can build up a quick affinity and a lasting relationship.

Key Takeaway

1) First is the last impression—make an everlasting first impression

2) Dress up well—get noticed.

3) Starting the conversation, "Breaking the Ice"—Either Either introduce yourself or take forward existing discussion

4) Boast without boasting—relate an incident from your past and compare it with your present position

5) Be the storyteller—Successful people, while talking in social gatherings, invariably have one or two incredible stories up in their sleeves

6) Open yourself up, open up your hearts, and share your inner feelings, understand each other's vulnerability and build a long-lasting relationship

7) Encourage another person to talk about themselves—people like to talk about themselves. "Self-disclosure is extra rewarding."

8) Similarity breeds likeability. We prefer those people or things with something in common.

9) Travel, compliments, and Advice are the most favoured topics for initiating quick responses

10) Stir up passion—When speaking with feelings and emotions, we draw greater attention and arouse interest

Chapter Eleven

Improving Social Skills

Mastering the Art of Social Skills

"Public speaking is the number-one fear
... even over death!"
-Emily Deschanel.

When you want to succeed in life, no money can help you buy networking skills. You can only have an effective network by gradually building it thoughtfully. If you succeed in building a network, you can rise in life; your career graph can sour, and achieve your life goals. However, you can have network only if you have mastered the art of social skills.

Let us understand what social skills are? To many people, vaguely, it means talking or interacting intelligently or constructively in different social groups. If you are a loner and feel awkward amid social groups and find it hard to initiate a talk with a new set of people in more contemporary settings, it may affect how you get on with your life and career. One must bear in mind that struggling with social skills is not similar to being unsocial.

However, you can improve your social skills by following the ten strategies as stated hereunder. By following these strategies, one can learn to be part of the social milieu by knowing its norms and behavioural etiquette.

1. Act normally and talk to new people

Even when you do not feel like talking to new people, force yourself to go out to speak to a diverse group of people. It would help if you did not let anxiety and apprehension hold you back from starting a talk. Initially, you will loath the idea, but gradually become accustomed to it and start liking it.

2. Take baby steps initially

If you do not want to go to social networking gatherings and parties right away, take small steps initially, such as going out to a grocery store or a restaurant and starting a small talk with the cashier like saying "Thank you." When you practice making small talk, you gradually overcome your nervousness and stop being shy talking to new people.

3. Set up a goal for yourself

Try to enrol yourself in a social activity for like-minded people or join a hobby class or social skill support group where you would meet new people and make new friends. By doing this, you would be enlarging your social circle to allow more interaction.

4. Offer greetings liberally

When you profusely greet a person, you open a wide possibility of initiating the talk. Listen attentively to the person you have greeted, encouraging him to talk about himself and find scope to put open-ended questions to keep the conversation going steady. Besides, when you welcome someone, you make his day.

What goes around comes around. It would soon turn viral as everyone starts greeting the other person in town, a complete game-changer for everyone. When we admire someone genuinely, it leads them to new heights of creativity. The small admiration they receive will help give them space to think more imaginatively and perceive things from a different and holistic point of view.

5. Greetings emanating from the heart lay the foundation of a strong friendship

When genuine respect comes straight from the heart, it triggers recognition and acknowledgement. It ignites a flare in a person's heart, believing that he has been recognized. It then helps the person to change from a shy and introverted into a person of self-assurance who could turn out to be your trusted friend for all times to come.

And the more we try and help others go out of their cocoon, the more we allow ourselves to build a secure social network. When you help in spreading happiness, happiness comes back to you. When we praise, it makes the person who gets it and the person who extends, both happy. Positive vibes emanate from both persons, positively impacting each other.

6. Follow Good Etiquette

Good etiquette and mannerism go a long way in showing that you are thorough with social skills. Courtesy, graciousness, and civility, along with table manners, help a person establish his social credentials.

7. Non-verbal communication

When we do not talk, we still communicate through our body language. An enlightened person can read what is going on in our minds simply by observing our body language. Hence, when we are not speaking, we should be relaxed, calm, and stress-free, making excellent eye contact, genuinely and attentively listening, and giving timely and relevant inputs to the conversation.

8. Read and be up-to-date on current events

It would help if you were thorough with the current events and what is majorly happening around the globe. It shows that you are an enlightened person. Topics on politics and religions are best avoided and not broached as they infringe on the controversy. Topics of general interest are a great way to initiate a conversation.

9. **Make positive affirmations**

In the back of your mind, make positive affirmations that you are doing great on social skills and likely to contribute a great deal when attending any social gathering or parties. Positive affirmations play a significant role in building up a cheerful makeover. The positive thought is likely to bring you up on your confidence scale.

10. **"No road is long when in good company"- A Turkish Proverb**

Man is a social creature and always seeks companionship. When in company adopting to social skills are a must. It is essential to identify the problem when faced with difficulty in adopting social skills. After all, social skill helps people understand each other better and have intimate bonding, leading to a better society.

Key Take Away

1)Succeed in life by practising networking skills and mastering the art of social skills

2)What are social skills- It is being able to talk or interact intelligently or constructively in different social groups.

3)Act normally and speak to new people, not let anxiety and apprehension hold you back from starting a talk

4)Take baby steps initially, such as going out to a grocery store or a restaurant and starting a small conversation with the cashier. Set up a goal for yourself by enlarging your social circle where there will be scope for more interactions

5)Offer greetings liberally - you open a wide possibility of initiating the talk and encouraging him to talk about himself.

6)Greetings emanating from the heart lay the foundation of a solid friendship. True respect comes straight from the heart.

It triggers recognition and acknowledgement, showing that you are thorough with social skills and what goes around comes around.

7)Follow Good Etiquette: Good etiquette and mannerism go a long way in showing that you are thorough with social skills.

8)A non-verbal communication: An enlightened person can read what is going on in our minds by observing our body language.

9)Read and be up-to-date on current events -This shows that you are an enlightened person.

10)Make positive affirmations -Positive affirmations play a significant role in building a cheerful makeover.

11)"No road is long when in good company"- A Turkish Proverb-Man is a social creature; he always seeks companionship.

Chapter Twelve

Influence Audience with Ease by Speaking as a Fearless and Passionate Speaker

Teach Your Listeners Comprehensively

"The best way to conquer stage fright is to know what you're talking about."
— Michael H Mescon.

Subject experts can express themselves freely and with enthusiasm while communicating verbally. We become expert speakers who speak overpoweringly only after discovering our core subject on which one is special, and in most cases, it comes with due practice. They are two things that sets apart a gifted presenter from an average orator.

However, passion should be used at times only while making a speech and just in the right quantity. Being too passionate can spoil any good address. Too much excitement in speech will likely overshadow facts, and the audience loses touch with the message. Speaking for a living is not an easy task; we can learn to talk with enthusiasm if we consider a few guidelines given below:

1. Use of broad words

Use of the word "we" instead of "you" indicates that we, as subject experts are eager to take on more and more people who are keen to learn to speak with passion. It suggests that we, as a presenter, are ready to teach our listeners comprehensively.

2. Stay on course with the listeners

When communicating, it is essential to receive visual signals from the viewers to know if they are on the same page with the presenter. We should know how and when to change gears while speaking to maintain an on-course passage with them. We should know about the listeners' awareness level and their background to make a direct connection with them. We should ensure that the listeners are with you and not disinterested in your speech as it serves no purpose.

3. **Be your natural self**

While on stage, you should also let your personality do the talking. Let your listeners believe you are truthful about what you are talking about. Interacting with viewers frequently works wonders. Get them to speak in between and seek questions. Reward them with your admiration; make them feel elevated and happy. They are keen to know not only about your knowledge but also about your personality.

4. **Speak with authority**

While you are on stage, many people have come to listen to you. They all have some expectations from you as they believe that they will learn something new today. All of this should not make you nervous or frightful instead, believing in yourself, you should talk with confidence and authority and as a subject expert. Mix some humour in between to liven up the speech.

5. **Be an enthusiastic master storyteller**

We have all loved stories ever since we were toddlers. You may start your speech by revealing why you have opted to be here on stage. Show your spectators that they can relate to you as a presenter and interact. Be a reliable person whose stories the audience can easily relate to and be motivated by. And when stories are told with passion, it works wonders.

Enthusiasm is infectious. If we speak with confidence, it affects the listeners directly, and they are willing to ignore all our other imperfections and shortcomings as orators.

6. **Making noticeable movement on stage**

Some deliberate movements by the orator add sparkle to the effects on the viewers. But not too often, but occasionally, as the presenter takes one step closer to the listeners or through his hand gestures, he drives his point to the viewers in a much more effective way.

However, caution should be observed in making such body movements by the orator so that the listeners are not distracted from the speech's core message.

7. Speak in a commanding voice

Speaking in a passionately commanding voice captures the audience's attention. The tone of voice can go up or low depending on the requirements of the speech. Sometimes particular emphasis to an idea can be accorded simply by saying it in a soft or low tone. There is no point in getting too emotional, as it can sharpen your style. The audience may not listen to you, simply because you became too emotional.

8. Speaking in high- and low-pitched tones

While preparing the content of what you will say on the stage, make a side note of all the stories and anecdotes you will reveal while also mentioning the hard facts and information. All the stories and accounts can be said in a high tone while restricting the hard facts to soft and low-pitched tones. It is one of the many approaches to having the viewers connected.

A proper mix of high and low voice techniques when delivering a passionate speech, along with a steady voice for the factual, will undoubtedly shore up the audience's attention.

9. **Clear message**

It is alright at times to speak with passion. However, it is not okay to talk with sentiments. The audience, then, might lose attention and focus on what is being said and how it is being said. There should be continuity and linkages to all the facts told in a speech. One chain of thought should follow another most logically and naturally.

A clear message should be derived from the address, which can be a clear takeaway for the audience. If the listeners follow the speaker from the start to the end of the speech, it is like a lost person being hand held from the rescue place to the area of his final destination.

10. **Work hard and do not get overwhelmed by negativities**

You have to devote your time and energy to your speech. You have to work hard (get up early morning, work during the day and get up even during the night to write notes about the new ideas) until you get it right for the next appearance on stage.

You have great content and have practiced well. Do not be too caring about others' opinions on what they will say about your speech. Develop a thick skin. Do not allow yourself to be overwhelmed by the thought of what others are going to say about your presentation.

Key Take Away

1) Subject experts can express themselves freely and with enthusiasm.

2) Use of the broad word "we" instead of "you."

3) Stay on course with the listeners; it is essential to receive visual signals from the viewers to know if they are on the same page with the presenter.

4) Be your natural self—let your personality do the talking.

5) While you are on stage, many people have come to listen to you. They all have some expectations from you, as they believe that they will learn something new today.

6) Be an enthusiastic master storyteller—and when stories are told with passion, it works wonders.

7) Enthusiasm is infectious

8) Make noticeable movements on stage.

Some deliberate actions by the orator add sparkle to the effects on the viewers.

9) Speak in a commanding voice.

Speaking in a passionately commanding voice captures the audience's attention.

10) Speak in high- and low-pitched tones.

All the stories and anecdotes can be told in high fashion while restricting the hard facts to soft and low pitch tones.

11) Have a Clear Message.

There should be continuity and linkages to all the facts said in a speech.

12) Work hard and do not get overwhelmed by negativities.

You have to devote your time and energy to your speech.

CHAPTER FOURTEEN

HAVING PERSUASIVE COMMUNICATION SKILL

BE AN ACCOMPLISHED IN VERBAL SKILL

"It takes one hour of preparation for each minute of presentation time."
– *Wayne Burgraff.*

Giving a good talk comes after repeated practice, as talking in front of a crowd is not an ordinary act as it is with eating, sleeping, walking, fighting, or even playing games. Giving an impactful talk depends on how accomplished you are in verbal skills. It is only possible when the orator and the listener are open, and there is a direct connection between the two.

In other words, the orator has to seek the viewer's undivided attention, and the viewer has to give the presenter his complete concentration. It will pave the way for a heartfelt or passionate, open connection between the two, leading to smooth two-way messages.

One can make a great talk if the orator is fired up with a desire to change how the world looks at an issue. The orator who strongly believes in what he will tell his viewers will flourish as a presenter. We have seen instances where great orators have altered the course of history by delivering an impactful talk. (More about it in the preceding chapter: How Legendary speakers impacted the world?)

If we are to talk publicly on any issue, we have to research and prepare our content to positively affect the people sitting in front of us in some form or the other. It may create powerful and direct connections between the orator and the listener, leading to a meaningful and worthwhile discussion.

Before preparing the content of any talk, the presenter may ask two questions with himself i.e. 1) Is it going to impact the listener's life in any way, and 2) Do I, as an orator, firmly believe in what I will say to my viewers. If the answer to both is a strong YES, there is every likelihood of the talk being powerful and impactful.

Remember the first four minutes of your talk remains the most crucial period. During this period, the listener's engagement level is open to the orator, and he must do everything to grab his undivided attention. Hence every talk must be preceded by first establishing a rapport with the listeners by grabbing their attention and then introducing the topic.

1. Speaking convincingly and conversationally

People try to engage in persuasive speaking most of the time in their daily lives. Be it a sales pitch by a salesman to a prospective client, promoting an idea in a corporate presentation, or putting up an argument in a board-level meeting. Or even trying to convince an unrelenting mom by her daughter for permission to go on a solo hitch hiking trip in a foreign country. In this type of presentation, the orator must meet the listener halfway down the line of his understanding.

The speaker first has to assess the audience's level of knowledge and intellectuality. By combining the three essential elements of a convincing speech, i.e. , ethos(credibility), logos (logic), and pathos (emotions), can enhance the apparent influence. Any successful speaker first tries to establish a strong ethos and then introduce pathos and logos in his argument to win over his listeners.

Speaking to the listeners in a conversational mode rather than the speech mode has a better effect. All great orators ensure that they speak conversationally and with honesty. They do this to have the minds and hearts of their audience responding to it more impactfully.

2. Know your listeners

It is good to know about your listeners' profiles before making the presentation. By knowing their profiles, you may include and address their concerns in your presentation. It will pre-empt any negative response from them. By addressing the audience's concerns, the orator succeeds in winning over most of his viewers.

The orator generally will sign off his persuasive presentation by calling his listeners to follow his line of thinking and asking them to take a particular line of action.

3. Make a surprising disclosure and speak through your body language

The orator generally catches the viewers' attention by making a stunning disclosure, which may be an eye-popping and attention-grabbing technique. The opening statement of the speech should be so startling (could also be statistics), which could raise the audience's emotions at various levels.

All good orators know how to convey their message through their body language which is a significant source of non-verbal communication. Looking well-mannered and upright and giving knowledgeable content are some of the traits of persuasive orators.

4. Relive an individual story

Viewers' empathy is drawn by the orator when in his opening statement, he relives an interesting short personal story that is relevant to the context in which he is speaking. It is, in most cases, lapped up by the listeners. By relating a personal story to the audience, the orator can visually and emotionally draw up his viewers' attention.

By sharing one's personal experiences and life's journey (could be some pleasant and positive experience bordering on humour), the orator starts to gain the undivided attention and allegiance of the listeners while also winning over their hearts and minds for all times to come.

5. Start with all persistent issues and relive with truthful thoughts.

Some orators describe an all persistently complex issue or problem to engage the viewer's attention. These problems can be easily identifiable and relatable by the listeners. Viewers' attention or empathy is earned by the orator immediately at the start of his talk. Why's and How's are some of the questions that may try to seek their answer.

Like all good actors, all good orators try to build a sense of truth for a more significant impact upon their viewers while delivering their message. The orators, when underlining a crucial point in their talk, just like the actors, have to be completely immersed into their role, emotionally, physically, and mentally. It will then lead to having a profound effect upon the viewers

6. **Opening with a famous quotation and summing up during intervals.**

An orator can draw the attention of his listeners by opening his talk by citing a famous quotation. In this way, he can inspire the imagination of his audience by keeping the quote relevant to his word. It is better to pause before and after the section in the talk. It is to underline the importance and for his viewers to understand it.

To ensure that the listeners' engagement level is maintained at all times, the orator may sum up what has been just said or ask his viewers to repeat what has been just spoken.

7. **Use of unconventional prop or emotion**

The use of unexpected and unconventional props is another way of seeking the viewers' attention and leaving behind a memorable talk, provided it is kept out of the view of the audience and shown only at the appropriate time. Some good orators also attempt to grab their viewers' attention by starting with an emotional appeal or pitch.

8. **Using factual information and answering "why."**

By citing actual and real-time data and facts along with its source of information, the orator can make his arguments quite convincing and logical and is easily understood by his listener. Good orators in their oration try to answer the question "why". "Why is this needed to discuss this topic over here?". It is another way to seek listeners' attention from the very start of the talk.

9. Using easily understood language and making eye contact

The orator must talk in a commoner's language that is easily understood by his viewers, leaving aside all the technical and scientific jargon. The orator must also use short sentences in his talk to make it easy for his listener. Making direct eye contact with the viewers also ensures an honest connection.

10. Call to action

All persuasive orations end with a call to action. Be it a product sale or a call to vote for the candidate, all the speeches sign off by some actionable point. For doing just that, it is best to start your presentation from end to start.

The last slide, which is the final goal of the exhibition, should be made first, so that there is no danger of wandering off while giving details in the middle slides. Hence, the final objective or the goal of the presentation should be written first. Then the mid portion, and finally focus on the introduction.

Key Take Away

1)Giving an impactful talk depends on how accomplished you are in verbal skills. One can make a great talk if the orator is fired up with a desire to change how the world looks at an issue.

2)It may create powerful and direct connections between the orator and the listener, leading to a meaningful and worthwhile discussion.

3)Know your listener and their profiles before making the presentation

4)The first four minutes of the talk remain the most crucial period, achieved by speaking convincingly and conversationally by first establishing a rapport with the listeners by grabbing their attention and then introducing the topic.

5)Make a surprising disclosure and speak through your body language

6)The viewers' attention is generally caught early by the orator by making a startling disclosure.

7)Viewers draw empathy by describing an interesting short personal story relevant to the context.

8)Start with all persistent issues and relive with truthful thought-To engage the viewer, some orators start to describe a persistently complex issue or problem.

9)Opening with a famous quotation and summing up during intervals-An orator can draw the attention of his listeners by opening his talk by citing a favourite quote.

10)Use of unconventional prop or emotion- To seek the viewers' attention.

11)Using basic information and answering "why"-Good orators in their oration try to answer the question "why".

12)Using easily understood language and making eye contact-The orator must talk in a commoner's language that is easily understood by his viewers, leaving aside all the technical and scientific jargon

13)All persuasive orations end with a call to action.

Chapter Fifteen

SUSTAINING AN ELOQUENT MINDSET FOR LONG-TERM SUCCESS

JOURNEY TOWARDS CULTIVATING AN ELOQUENT MINDSET

"They may forget what you said, but they will never forget how you made them feel."
— *Carl W. Buechner.*

During one of my soul-searching adventures, I found myself traversing the majestic terrains of the Himalayas, seeking solace in the serenity of nature. It was during this expedition that I stumbled upon a quaint village nestled amid the verdant hills, and it was here that my journey towards cultivating an eloquent mindset truly began.

In this secluded village, I was fortunate to encounter an elderly villager, revered for his profound wisdom and captivating storytelling. Eager to unravel the secrets of his eloquence, I sought his guidance. Perched on a moss-covered rock, the old man welcomed me with a warm smile and a steaming cup of masala chai, a quintessential Indian gesture of hospitality.

His first lesson on cultivating an eloquent mindset came in the form of a poignant tale about a humble gardener. He narrated how this unassuming soul had transformed a barren patch of land into a blooming oasis with his meticulous care and deliberate choice of words. Through this parable,

I realized that eloquence is not merely about the complexity of language but about the profound impact that carefully selected words can have on the hearts and minds of listeners.

Eager to delve deeper, I immersed myself in the daily rhythm of life within the village. I discovered that despite their simple lifestyles, the villagers possessed a unique eloquence in their interactions.

168

Whether sharing local folklore or discussing the day's harvest, their narratives were laced with vivid imagery and genuine emotion. Their eloquence stemmed from their authentic connection to their surroundings and their shared experiences as a community.

As the sun dipped behind the snow-capped peaks, the old man conducted enchanting storytelling sessions in the village square. Mesmerized by his ability to weave magic with words, I realized that effective communication lies at the heart of eloquence.

The old man emphasized the importance of active listening and empathy, stressing how understanding one's audience fosters the creation of narratives that deeply resonate with them.

Moreover, during my stay in the village, I encountered a band of wandering musicians whose harmonious melodies appeared to surpass language, stirring emotions that words frequently find difficult to convey. Inspired by their ability to communicate without words, I came to understand that eloquence surpasses verbal language, speaking directly to the soul and transcending cultural boundaries.

As my days in the village drew to a close, I bid farewell to the elderly person and the kind-hearted villagers, carrying with me a wealth of insights and a renewed sense of purpose. I understood that an eloquent mindset thrives on continuous learning, an appreciation for the subtleties of language, and a genuine connection to the human experience.

Armed with the wisdom of the eloquent gardener, the heartfelt narratives of the villagers, and the soul-stirring melodies of the musicians, I returned to my home town, determined to infuse these profound lessons into my writing.

With a newfound understanding of the intricate tapestry of eloquence, I set out to pen my next literary masterpiece, aiming to evoke emotions, stir imaginations, and leave an indelible mark on the hearts of my readers worldwide.

Eloquence is the ability to communicate fluently

Eloquence is the ability to communicate fluently and persuasively, using language in a clear and concise manner. It is a skill that can be learned and honed over time, and it is one that can be essential for success in many different fields.

An eloquent mindset is one that is focused on clear and effective communication. It is a mindset that values the power of words and the importance of using them wisely. People with an eloquent mindset are constantly striving to improve their communication skills, and they are always looking for new ways to express themselves more effectively.

Sustaining an eloquent mindset for long-term success is essential. In today's fast-paced world, we are constantly bombarded with information, and it is more important than ever to be able to communicate our ideas clearly and effectively. An eloquent mindset can help us to stand out from the crowd and achieve our goals.

Benefits of an Eloquent Mindset

There are many benefits to having an eloquent mindset. For one, it can help you to communicate more effectively with others.

This can be important in both personal and professional settings. For example, if you are able to communicate your ideas clearly and concisely to your boss, you are more likely to get what you want. Similarly, if you are able to communicate effectively with your customers, you are more likely to build strong relationships and generate sales.

An eloquent mindset can also   help you to become a more confident and persuasive person. When you are able to express yourself clearly and concisely, you are more likely to be taken seriously and to have your ideas respected. This can be especially important in situations where you are trying to convince others to see things your way.

Finally, an eloquent mindset can help you to become a more successful person. In today's economy, communication skills are more important than ever before. Employers are looking for people who can communicate effectively in a variety of settings. If you have an eloquent mindset, you will be more likely to get hired and promoted.

How to Sustain an Eloquent Mindset

There are a few things you can do to sustain an eloquent mindset for long-term success:

Be mindful of your language. Pay attention to the words you use and the way you use them. Choose your words carefully and avoid using clichés or jargon.

Be clear and concise.

Get to the point quickly and avoid using unnecessary words. Be active and engaged. When you are communicating, make eye contact, speak clearly, and use gestures to emphasize your points.

Another study by the University of California, Berkeley found that people who are able to communicate their ideas clearly and concisely are more likely to be successful in job interviews and salary negotiations.

Be open to feedback.

Ask others for feedback on your communication skills and be willing to make changes.

Practice regularly.

The more you practice communicating, the better you will become at it.

Tips for Sustaining an Eloquent Mindset in the Long Term

Here are a few tips for sustaining an eloquent mindset in the long term:

<u>Read regularly.</u>

Reading is one of the best ways to improve your vocabulary and learn new ways to express yourself.

<u>Write regularly.</u>

Writing is another great way to improve your communication skills. Try to write something every day, even if it is just a few sentences.

<u>Listen actively.</u>

When you are listening to others, pay attention to what they are saying and try to understand their point of view.

<u>Be mindful of your body language.</u>

Your body language can communicate just as much as your words. Make eye contact, smile, and stand up straight when you are communicating.

Be yourself.

Don't try to be someone you're not.

People will be able to tell if you are being genuine, and they will be more likely to trust you and respect you.

Be aware of your audience.

Tailor your communication style to the people you are talking to. For example, you would communicate differently with your boss than you would with your friends.

Be respectful.
Even if you disagree with someone , you can still communicate with them in a respectful manner. Avoid using personal attacks or name-calling.

Be open-minded.

Be willing to listen to other people's ideas, even if they differ from your own.

<u>Be humble.</u>

Don't act like you know everything. Be willing to learn from others.

<u>Conclusion</u>

There is a growing body of research that supports the benefits of an eloquent mindset.

For example, not long ago , a study by the University of Minnesota found that people who are more articulate are more likely to be perceived as intelligent and competent.

A recent study by the University of Pennsylvania found that people who are able to build strong relationships with their colleagues are more likely to be promoted and to earn higher salaries.

If you're looking to achieve your goals and succeed in all areas of your life, I encourage you to develop an eloquent mindset. By following the tips above, you can learn to communicate more effectively and persuasively.

Sustaining an eloquent mindset for long-term success is essential. By following the tips above, you can develop and maintain the communication skills you need to succeed in all areas of your life.

By following these tips, you can develop and maintain an eloquent mindset that will help you to achieve your goals and succeed in all areas of your life.

Integrating Effective Communication Practices into Your Daily Life

Effective communication is essential for success in all areas of life. Whether you're trying to build relationships, close a deal, or simply get your point across, being able to communicate clearly and effectively is key.

Here are a few tips on how to integrate effective communication practices into your daily life:

Be mindful of your audience. Tailor your communication style to the people you're talking to.

For example, you would communicate differently with your boss than you would with your friends.

Be clear and concise. Get to the point quickly and avoid using unnecessary words. A study by the University of Minnesota found that people who are more articulate are more likely to be perceived as intelligent and competent.

Another study by the University of California, Berkeley found that people who are able to communicate their ideas c learly and concisely are more likely to be successful in job interviews and salary negotiations.

<u>Be active and engaged</u>. When you're communicating, make eye contact, speak clearly, and use gestures to emphasize your points.

<u>Be open to feedback</u>. Ask others for feedback on your communication skills and be willing to make changes.

<u>Practice regularly.</u> The more you practice communicating, the better you will become at it.

<u>How I've integrated effective communication practices into my daily life:-</u>

At work, I always make sure to tailor my communication style to my audience. For example, when I'm giving a presentation to senior leadership, I use more formal language and avoid using slang. When I'm talking t o my team members, I use a more casual tone and I'm more likely to use contractions.

In my personal life, I make sure to be clear and concise when I'm communicating with my friends and family. I know that they're busy, so I don't want to waste their time.

I also make sure to be active and engaged when I'm communicating.

I make eye contact, speak clearly, and use gestures to emphasize my points. I want to make sure that the people I'm talking to are paying attention and that they understand what I'm saying.

I'm also open to feedback on my communication skills. I know that I can always improve, so I appreciate when people are willing to give me feedback.

Finally, I practice communicating regularly. I read books and articles on communication, I watch videos, and I take classes. I want to make sure that I'm always developing my communication skills.

As you can see, there are many benefits to integrating effective communication practices into your daily life. If you're looking to achieve your goals and succeed in all areas of life, I encourage you to make communication a priority.

Here are a few additional tips for integrating effective communication practices into your daily life:

- **<u>Start your day by thinking about your communication goals</u>.** What do you want to achieve in your interactions with others? Once you know your goals, you can tailor your communication accordingly.

- **<u>Be mindful of your body language</u>.** Your body language can communicate just as much as your words. Make eye contact, smile, and stand up straight when you're communicating.

- **<u>Be a good listener</u>.** When you're listening to someone, pay attention to what they're saying and try to understand their point of view. This will help you to communicate more effectively with them.

- **<u>Be respectful</u>.** Even if you disagree with someone, you can still communicate with them in a respectful manner. Avoid using personal attacks or name-calling.

- **<u>Be open-minded</u>.** Be willing to listen to other people's ideas, even if they differ from your own.

- **<u>Be yourself</u>.** Don't try to be someone you're not. People can tell when you're being genuine, and they're more likely to trust and respect you if you are.

By following these tips, you can learn to communicate more effectively and persuasively in all areas of your life.

Key Take away

1. **<u>Eloquence is about Clear and Effective Communication</u>:** Eloquence involves expressing yourself fluently and persuasively, using simple language that is easy to understand. It's not about using complex words, but rather about getting your point across in a way that resonates with others.

2. **<u>Being   Mindful of Language and Clarity</u>:**
Pay attention   to the words you use and how
you use them. Choose your words carefully,
avoiding clichés or overly complicated language. Be clear and to the point, getting your
message across without unnecessary words.

3. **<u>Active   Listening and Empathy</u>**: Effective
communication isn't just about speaking; it
also involves listening actively and understanding the perspective of the person you're talking
to. This helps in tailoring your message to better resonate with your audience.

4. **<u>Body Language Matters</u>**: Your body language
communicates as much as your words do.

Make eye contact, smile, and stand up straight when
you're communicating to show that you're engaged and
attentive.

1. **<u>Continual L earning and Practice</u>:** The
more you practice communicating, the better you become at it. Read regularly to improve your vocabulary, write daily to hone your
communication skills, and be open to feedback
from others to make necessary improvements.

2. **<u>Respect, Open-Mindedness, and Authen-</u>**

<u>**ticity**</u>: Respect others even in disagreement, be open to diverse perspectives, and remain true to yourself. Genuine communication fosters trust and respect from others.

3. <u>**Setting Communication Goals:**</u> Begin your day with a clear idea of what you aim to communicate and achieve in your interactions with others.

Tailor your communication style accordingly to ensure effective transmission of your message.

8. <u>**Benefits of Effective Communication**</u>: Effective communication can improve how others perceive you, enhancing your chances of success both personally and professionally.

It can help build strong relationships, promote understanding, and facilitate success in various endeavors.

By incorporating these practices into your daily life, you can improve your communication skills and, consequently, enhance your ability to achieve your goals and succeed in various aspects of your life.

Remember, effective communication is not just about the words you speak, but also about how you express yourself and connect with others.

BEFORE YOU GO

ENJOYED THIS BOOK?
Your review helps more readers discover this book and
supports independent authors.
Please take 30 seconds to leave an honest review on
Amazon.
[Scan the QR code here.]

QR Code

Or

Click or visit the link given (https://relinks.me/B0GX 2Z3HFD.) here
Thank you for your support!
— Manjul Tewari

188

Scan this. QR code

INTRODUCTION

Mahatma Gandhi, Nelson Mandela, and Martin Luther King Jr. are some of the most iconic figures in modern history who have demonstrated remarkable resilience and the Phoenix Factor. These three individuals faced numerous obstacles and challenges, yet remained steadfast in their beliefs and principles, and ultimately achieved social and political change through nonviolent resistance.

Mahatma Gandhi, born in 1869 in Porbandar, India, grew up in a devout Hindu family. Despite being a bright student, he struggled to find his place in the world, feeling lost and directionless. However, after moving to London to study law, Gandhi became exposed to the ideas of non-violent resistance, which would become the cornerstone of his political and social philosophy.

Upon returning to India, Gandhi became actively involved in the Indian independence movement, advocating for peaceful resistance and civil disobedience as a means of achieving freedom from British rule. He became known for his signature tactics, such as hunger strikes and public protests, which were often met with violence and repression by the British authorities.

Despite facing numerous setbacks and challenges, Gandhi remained resolute in his convictions, refusing to compromise his principles or resort to violence. He spent a total of seven years in prison for his beliefs, enduring harsh treatment and isolation.

However, it was during his time in prison that Gandhi truly demonstrated the Phoenix Factor. He used his incarceration as an opportunity to reflect on his beliefs and values, writing extensively on his philosophy of non-violence and developing strategies for achieving social and political change.

Gandhi's resilience and commitment to non-violence ultimately paid off, as he played a key role in the Indian independence movement and helped lead India to freedom in 1947. He continued to work tirelessly for social and political change until his assassination in 1948, leaving behind a legacy of peaceful resistance and non-violent protest that continues to inspire activists and leaders around the world today.

Nelson Mandela, born in 1918 in a small village in the Transkei region of South Africa, grew up under the oppressive system of apartheid, which institutionalized racial segregation and discrimination against black South Africans. Despite facing numerous obstacles in his early life, Mandela was a gifted student and went on to study law at the University of Witwatersrand in Johannesburg. He soon became involved in the anti-apartheid movement, joining the African National Congress (ANC) in 1944.

Mandela's activism led to his arrest in 1962 and subsequent imprisonment for 27 years. During this time, he endured brutal treatment and was subjected to hard labour and solitary confinement. However, Mandela's spirit remained unbroken. He used his time in prison to study, write, and reflect on his beliefs and values.

Finally, in 1990, Mandela was released from prison and began negotiating with the government to end apartheid. Despite facing resistance and opposition from some quarters, Mandela persisted in his efforts and ultimately succeeded in bringing an end to the racist system. In 1994, Mandela was elected as the first black President of South Africa in the country's first democratic elections. During his presidency, he worked tirelessly to build a new, more equal South Africa, promoting reconciliation and forgiveness between the country's different racial groups.

Throughout his life, Nelson Mandela demonstrated incredible resilience and the Phoenix Factor. Despite facing immense adversity and hardship, he remained true to his principles and beliefs. He used his experiences to become a stronger and more determined leader, never losing sight of his ultimate goal: to create a better world for all people, regardless of race, ethnicity, or background.

Martin Luther King Jr., born in 1929 in Atlanta, Georgia, grew up in a deeply segregated society. He experienced discrimination and racism first hand, but he was determined to fight for a better future for himself and for his fellow African Americans.

Another example of the power of resilience and the Phoenix Factor is derived from the life of Martin Luther King Jr. He is one of the most famous civil rights leaders in history, known for his unwavering commitment to justice and equality. His life is a testament to the power of resilience and the Phoenix Factor, as he faced numerous challenges and setbacks, yet remained steadfast in his beliefs and principles.

King was born in 1929 in Atlanta, Georgia, and grew up in a deeply segregated society. He experienced discrimination and racism first-hand, but he was determined to fight for a better future for himself and for his fellow African Americans.

Throughout his life, King faced numerous challenges and setbacks. He was arrested and jailed on numerous occasions for his civil rights activism, and he faced violent opposition from those who opposed his message of nonviolent resistance. He endured physical attacks and verbal abuse, but he never wavered in his commitment to justice and equality.

Despite these challenges, King remained resilient and committed to his cause. He used his experiences to inspire and motivate others, delivering powerful speeches and organizing peaceful protests and demonstrations. He became a prominent figure in the civil rights movement, helping to bring about significant social and political change in the United States.

The Phoenix Factor was also evident in King's life, as he used his experiences to become a powerful voice for justice and equality. He was awarded the Nobel Peace Prize in 1964 for his nonviolent resistance to racial prejudice in America. His legacy continues to inspire people around the world, particularly those who fight for equality and justice.

The lives of Gandhi, Mandela, and King all demonstrate the power of resilience and the Phoenix Factor. These individuals faced immense obstacles and adversity in their lives, but they remained steadfast in their beliefs and refused to compromise their principles. Their unwavering commitment to non-violent resistance, justice, and equality has made them enduring symbols of hope and inspiration for people around the world.

Their lives are also a reminder that resilience is not simply a matter of gritting one's teeth and soldiering on in the face of adversity. Rather, resilience is a complex and multifaceted process that involves adapting to change, drawing on one's strengths and resources, and cultivating a sense of purpose and meaning in life.

Research has shown that resilience is not something that people either have or don't have; rather, it is something that can be cultivated and developed over time. This means that anyone can learn to be more resilient, regardless of their background or circumstances.

Some strategies that can help build resilience include:

1. Developing a strong social support network: Having a network of supportive friends and family members can help provide emotional support and practical assistance in times of need.

2. Practicing self-care: Taking care of one's physical and emotional health through activities such as exercise, meditation, and therapy can help build resilience and promote well-being.

3. Cultivating a sense of purpose and meaning: Setting goals and pursuing activities that are personally meaningful can help provide a sense of purpose and direction in life.

4. Learning from experience: Reflecting on past experiences and learning from both successes and failures can help build resilience and develop a sense of self-efficacy.

In conclusion, the lives of Gandhi, Mandela, and King serve as powerful examples of the potential for human resilience and the capacity for individuals to rise above even the most difficult of circumstances. Their legacies continue to inspire people around the world today, reminding us of the importance of resilience, determination, and the Phoenix Factor in achieving our goals and making a positive impact on the world.

Chapter 1: Building a Strong Foundation: The Importance of Self-Awareness and Self-Care

Self-awareness and self-care are critical components of building a strong foundation for a fulfilling and successful life. In a fast-paced world, individuals often focus on work and neglect their well-being, leading to burnout and serious health issues. However, prioritizing self-care and reflecting on our needs and desires is crucial to handling life's challenges, achieving our goals and aspirations, and maintaining strong relationships. Recent studies support the importance of self-awareness and self-care. Practicing mindfulness meditation can lead to significant reductions in symptoms of anxiety and depression, while self-care practices, such as physical activity, getting enough sleep, and stress management techniques, improve mental and physical health outcomes.

In addition, self-care practices can prevent and manage chronic diseases such as diabetes and heart disease.

Building self-awareness involves recognizing one's thoughts, feelings, and behaviours and understanding how they impact oneself and others. Self-care involves taking care of oneself physically and mentally by getting enough sleep, eating healthily, exercising regularly, and doing activities that bring joy. To build a strong foundation of self-awareness and self-care, individuals can start with self-reflection, identify their values and priorities, practice self-compassion, delegate work, set boundaries, and seek support from loved ones or professionals. Overall, building a strong foundation of self-awareness and self-care leads to increased happiness, fulfilment, and success in personal and professional lives.

Chapter 2- Embracing Change and Uncertainty: Developing Adaptability and Flexibility

This article highlights the importance of embracing change and uncertainty and developing adaptability and flexibility. The story of Anna serves as an example of how embracing change and uncertainty led her to a more fulfilling and rewarding career. Recent research supports the importance of adaptability and flexibility for success and well-being. Studies have found that individuals who exhibited higher levels of adaptability had better job satisfaction, fewer symptoms of burnout, and better emotional well-being. Developing adaptability and flexibility is not always easy, but it requires a mindset shift and a willingness to embrace new challenges and opportunities. Benefits of developing adaptability and flexibility include career advancement, better problem-solving skills, and increased resilience.

1. Adaptability and flexibility can improve our overall well-being by boosting our confidence and self-esteem, leading to better mental health outcomes, and reducing stress and burnout, leading to improved physical health.

2. Adaptability and flexibility can enhance our creativity by allowing us to approach challenges in new and innovative ways.

3. To cultivate adaptability and flexibility, it's important to embrace change and uncertainty, be open to new experiences, and develop resilience.

4. Improved Well-being Adaptability and flexibility can also improve our overall well-being. When we are able to adapt to new situations and overcome challenges, we feel a sense of accomplishment and satisfaction. This can boost our confidence and self-esteem, leading to bet-

ter mental health outcomes. Additionally, by being flexible in our approach, we can reduce stress and burnout, leading to improved physical health as well.

5. Enhanced Creativity Adaptability and flexibility can also enhance our creativity. When we are open to new experiences and ideas, we are more likely to think outside the box and come up with innovative solutions to problems. This can be a valuable asset in both our personal and professional lives, allowing us to approach challenges in new and creative ways.

Tips for Cultivating Adaptability and Flexibility

1. Embrace Change and Uncertainty: The first step to developing adaptability and flexibility is to embrace change and uncertainty. Instead of fearing the unknown, view it as an opportunity to learn and grow. Recognize that change is inevitable and that the ability to adapt to new situations is a valuable skill.

2. Be Open to New Experiences: To develop adaptability and flexibility, it's important to be open to new experiences. This can include trying new things, meeting new people, and ex-

ploring new ideas. By stepping outside of your comfort zone, you can expand your horizons and become more adaptable to change.

3. Develop Resilience: Resilience is the ability to bounce back from setbacks and challenges. To develop adaptability and flexibility, it's important to cultivate resilience. This can include practicing mindfulness, staying positive, and focusing on solutions instead of problems.

4. Continuously Learn and Grow: To be adaptable and flexible, it's important to continuously learn and grow. This can include seeking out new training and development opportunities, staying up-to-date with industry trends, and being open to feedback and constructive criticism.

5. Be Flexible in Your Approach: To be adaptable and flexible, it's important to be flexible in your approach. This can include being open to different perspectives, adjusting your strategy when necessary, and being willing to take risks. In conclusion, developing adaptability and flexibility is essential for success and well-being in today's fast-paced and rapidly changing world. By embracing change and uncertainty, being open to new experiences, de-

veloping resilience, continuously learning and growing, and being flexible in our approach, we can thrive in both our personal and professional lives. Let us take inspiration from Anna's story and commit to developing these valuable skills.

Chapter 3- Cultivating a Growth Mindset: The Key to Overcoming Challenges and Achieving Goals

Michael Jordan, who used setbacks as motivation to improve his skills and eventually became a legend in basketball. There are several scientific studies that support the idea that adopting a growth mindset can lead to improved academic performance, positive emotions, and greater well-being in the workplace.

A growth mindset is the belief that abilities and intelligence can be developed through hard work, dedication, and learning from mistakes. In contrast, a fixed mindset is the belief that abilities are innate and cannot be changed. People with a growth mindset view challenges and setbacks as opportunities for growth and learning, and they understand that mistakes are an essential part of the learning process. By embracing a growth mindset, individuals can experience benefits such as resilience, improved problem-solving skills, greater creativity, and increased motivation.

There are some practical tips for cultivating a growth mindset, such as embracing challenges, emphasizing effort and learning, and focusing on the process rather than the outcome. We may conclude by emphasizing the importance of adopting a growth mindset in personal and professional pursuits to lead a more fulfilling life.

There is a great deal of importance of a growth mindset in achieving success and well-being. By adopting a growth mindset and viewing challenges as opportunities for growth, individuals can overcome obstacles and achieve their goals.

Chapter 4- Harnessing the Power of Positive Thinking: The Science of Optimism and Resilience

Positive thinking, resilience, and optimism are powerful tools that can help individuals overcome challenges, improve mental health and wellbeing, and live happier lives. Scientific studies have shown that individuals who practice positive thinking and optimism are less likely to experience symptoms of depression and anxiety, are better able to cope with stress, and are more likely to recover from depression if they do experience it. Resilience is also key to promoting mental health and wellbeing, and is associated with lower levels of stress, anxiety, and depression, and higher levels of life satisfaction.

To cultivate positive thinking, individuals can practice gratitude, reframe negative thoughts, surround themselves with positive people, focus on solutions, and practice self-care. Practicing gratitude involves reflecting on the things you are grateful for each day, which can help shift your focus from what is wrong to what is right in your life. Reframing negative thoughts involves focusing on what is going well and what you can do to improve your situation, rather than dwelling on what is going wrong. Surrounding yourself with positive people involves spending time with those who uplift and inspire you, and seeking out social situations and communities that foster positivity and optimism. Focusing on solutions involves focusing on what you can do to overcome challenges and move forward, rather than dwelling on the problem itself. Finally, practicing self-care is essential to maintaining a positive and resilient mindset, and can involve activities such as exercise, meditation, and getting enough rest and sleep.

Overall, by harnessing the power of positive thinking, resilience, and optimism, individuals can develop the strength and determination needed to overcome any obstacle and achieve their dreams. These tools can help individuals to better cope with the challenges and stressors of life and enjoy greater happiness and fulfilment.

Chapter 5- Building Confidence and Self-Efficacy: Overcoming Self-Doubt and Fear

Let us discusses the importance of building confidence and self-efficacy in overcoming self-doubt and fear to achieve one's goals. It highlights Serena Williams' life story as an example of someone who refused to let self-doubt and fear hold her back and became one of the greatest tennis players of all time. It is suggested that building confidence and self-efficacy is not always easy, but it can be achieved by acknowledging our successes and strengths, setting realistic goals, and breaking them down into manageable steps.

The article also cites scientific research showing that building confidence and self-efficacy can have a significant impact on mental health and well-being, increasing overall sense of well-being and reducing symptoms of anxiety and depression. Overall, we should focus on over strengths and accomplishments and work to develop a positive self-image and mindset to increase our resilience, happiness, and overall well-being.

Another way to build self-efficacy is to learn from failure. Failure is a natural part of any learning process, and it can provide valuable lessons that can help us grow and improve. By reframing failure as an opportunity to learn and grow, we can develop a more positive mindset and increase our self-efficacy.

In addition to these strategies, seeking out support and feedback from others can also be helpful in building confidence and self-efficacy. By surrounding ourselves with positive and supportive people who believe in us and our abilities, we can receive the encouragement and validation we need to continue pursuing our goals.

Ultimately, building confidence and self-efficacy is an ongoing process that requires effort and dedication. It may not always be easy, and setbacks and challenges are inevitable. However, by staying committed to our goals and working to develop a positive mindset and belief in ourselves, we can overcome self-doubt and fear and achieve great success in our personal and professional lives.

In conclusion, building confidence and self-efficacy is essential for overcoming self-doubt and fear and achieving our goals. By believing in ourselves and our abilities, setting high goals, and persisting in the face of challenges, we can accomplish anything we set our minds to. The scientific research also supports the idea that building confidence and self-efficacy can have a significant impact on our mental health and well-being. With practice and persistence, we can develop the skills and mindset we need to build our confidence and overcome our fears, leading to a happier and more fulfilling life.

Chapter 6- The Art of Perseverance: Strategies for Pushing Through Adversity and Setbacks

Perseverance is a quality that allows individuals to push through adversity and setbacks and ultimately achieve their goals. The power of perseverance is illustrated in the story of Diana Nyad, who at the age of 64 became the first person to swim from Cuba to Florida without a shark cage. Nyad had attempted this feat four times before, but each time, she was forced to abandon her mission due to storms, jellyfish stings, and other challenges. Despite the setbacks, Nyad refused to give up on her dream and continued to train, make adjustments to her plan, and visualize herself completing the swim.

Nyad's story highlights several strategies for pushing through adversity and setbacks. One of these strategies is maintaining a positive attitude and focusing on goals even in the face of challenges. Another strategy is being flexible and willing to adjust plans as needed. Having a support system can also be critical when facing difficulties. Finally, it is important to stay committed to goals and not give up when facing setbacks or obstacles.

Recent research has shed light on the science behind perseverance and strategies for pushing through adversity. Studies have shown that resilience, or the ability to bounce back from adversity, is a skill that can be learned and developed over time. Individuals who view challenges as opportunities for growth rather than threats are more likely to persevere and succeed. Setting achievable goals, seeking support, practicing self-compassion, and cultivating a growth mindset are all effective strategies for building resilience and perseverance.

In summary, perseverance is a key quality for achieving success in life. Nyad's story demonstrates the power of perseverance and highlights several strategies for pushing through adversity. Recent research has further emphasized the importance of building resilience and cultivating a growth mindset for achieving success in the face of challenges. By staying committed, flexible, and positive, individuals can overcome obstacles and ultimately achieve their goals.

Chapter 7- Understanding and Managing Emotions: The Foundation of Emotional Intelligence

Let us discuss the importance of understanding and managing emotions as the foundation of emotional intelligence. Let us remind ourselves about the   story of John who learned to manage his emotions with the help of a therapist after he was passed over for a promotion at work. John recognized his initial reaction was not helpful and took a more proactive approach, leading to personal and professional growth. The article highlights the importance of emotional intelligence in personal and professional success with research to back up the claim. A 2019 study found that emotional intelligence was positively related to job satisfaction and organizational commitment, while another study found it was associated with better relationship satisfaction and lower levels of conflict in romantic relationships. Additionally, individuals who are better able to manage their emotions are less likely to experience stress and more likely to experience positive emotions like happiness and excitement.

Let us examine various studies that suggest emotional intelligence is important for personal well-being, job performance, and success in the workplace. For instance, a 2019 study found that employees with higher levels of emotional intelligence are more likely to have better job performance, particularly when it comes to job crafting. A 2020 study found that individuals with higher levels of emotional intelligence are less likely to experience burnout in their jobs, and a 2021 study found that individuals who engage in regular mindfulness practices are better able to regulate their emotions and experience higher levels of positive emotions.

To develop emotional intelligence, individuals should practice self-awareness and self-reflection regularly, seek feedback from others, and develop coping mechanisms and strategies for managing difficult emotions. Mindfulness practices, such as meditation or deep breathing exercises, can help individuals become more present and in tune with their emotions. Furthermore, individuals should learn to recognize and name their emotions, to pause before reacting impulsively, and to use strategies like deep breathing and self-reflection to manage their feelings. By doing so, they can make better decisions, avoid impulsive actions that may have negative consequences, and experience a wide range of benefits in various aspects of their lives.

In conclusion, emotional intelligence is a crucial skill that can determine success in both personal and professional aspects of life. Understanding and managing emotions is the foundation of emotional intelligence, and it's an essential skill for success in both personal and professional aspects of life. By developing this skill, individuals can improve their relationships, communication, and decision-making abilities. Emotional intelligence is a skill that can be developed over time with practice and effort.

Chapter 8 - Resilience in Relationships: Building Strong Connections and Navigating Conflict

Resilience in relationships is the ability to maintain strong connections despite the challenges and conflicts that arise. Resilient relationships are built on trust, respect, and open communication. It's about being able to bounce back from difficult situations and continue to build a strong connection with your partner. Resilience is important in relationships for several reasons. First, relationships are inherently challenging, and conflicts are bound to arise. By developing resilience in relationships, we can navigate these conflicts more effectively and come out stronger on the other side. Second, resilience is important for maintaining a strong emotional connection with our partner. When we are resilient, we are better able to handle the emotional ups and downs that come with any relationship.

Finally, resilience is important for our overall emotional wellbeing. When we have strong, resilient relationships, we feel more supported and connected to those around us. To build resilience in relationships, open communication, empathy, trust, gratitude, and support network building are essential. Additionally, navigating conflict in a healthy way, developing a deeper understanding of each other's needs and perspectives, and working together to overcome obstacles are key. Resilience in relationships is closely tied to positive relationship outcomes, including greater relationship satisfaction, intimacy, and perceptions of partner support. Couples can build greater resilience in their relationships by developing effective communication strategies, navigating conflict in healthy ways, and maintaining a positive outlook.

Practice forgiveness: Forgiveness is an important aspect of building resilience in relationships. It's important to acknowledge and apologize for any mistakes or wrongdoings, and to forgive your partner when they do the same. Focus on the present: When conflicts arise, it's easy to get caught up in the past or worry about the future. Instead, try to focus on the present moment and work together with your partner to find a solution. Take breaks: If conflicts become heated or overwhelming, it's important to take a break and come back to the conversation when you are both calmer and more focused. Seek outside help: If you are struggling to navigate conflict or build resilience in your relationship, don't be afraid to seek outside help from a therapist or counsellor.

In summary, resilience is a crucial skill for maintaining strong and healthy relationships. It allows us to navigate conflict and challenges, and bounce back from difficult situations. By practicing open communication, developing trust, practicing empathy, cultivating gratitude, building a support network, and navigating conflict in healthy ways, we can build greater resilience in our relationships and achieve long-term satisfaction and happiness.

Chapter 9 - Finding Meaning and Purpose: The Role of Resilience in Living a Fulfilling Life

Resilience is a crucial factor in finding meaning and purpose in life. Let us take a look at the story of Bryan Stevenson, a lawyer and social justice activist, and how his resilience and sense of purpose have driven him to make positive change despite facing significant opposition and setbacks. Let us examine several recent studies that explore the role of resilience in finding meaning and purpose in life. These studies found that resilience played a significant role in mediating the relationship between stress and meaning in life, and individuals with higher levels of resilience reported higher levels of eudemonic well-being.

It is therefore suggested that resilience is a key factor in finding meaning and purpose in life, and that it may play a mediating role in the relationship between stress, adversity, and well-being. Let us conclude by discussing how resilience can help individuals find meaning and purpose in their lives by developing a sense of purpose, overcoming obstacles, and embracing new opportunities.

In addition, resilience can also help us develop a sense of gratitude and appreciation for the present moment. When we practice resilience, we learn to focus on the present and to appreciate the small things in life. This can help us cultivate a deeper sense of meaning and purpose in our daily lives.

How can we cultivate resilience? Resilience is a skill that can be developed through practice and effort. Here are some ways to cultivate resilience:

1. Practice mindfulness: Mindfulness is the practice of being present and aware of our thoughts, feelings, and sensations in the present moment. By practicing mindfulness, we can learn to observe our thoughts and emotions without judgement, which can help us develop a greater sense of resilience.

2. Cultivate positive thinking: Positive thinking involves focusing on the positive aspects of our lives, rather than dwelling on the negative. By cultivating a positive mindset, we can develop a sense of resilience and optimism.

3. Practice self-care: Self-care involves taking care of our physical, emotional, and mental health. By prioritizing self-care, we can develop greater resilience and better cope with stress and adversity.

4. Build a support network: Building a strong support network of family, friends, and other trusted individuals can help us develop greater resilience and provide us with the resources we need to overcome challenges and setbacks.

5. Develop a sense of purpose: Developing a sense of purpose involves identifying our values, passions, and goals, and working towards achieving them. By developing a sense of purpose, we can find greater meaning and fulfilment in our lives, which can contribute to our sense of resilience.

Conclusion: Finding meaning and purpose is an essential part of living a fulfilling life. However, this can be a difficult task, especially in the face of adversity and challenges.

Resilience is a key factor in helping individuals find and maintain a sense of purpose and fulfilment in their lives, even in the face of setbacks and difficulties.

By cultivating resilience through practices like mindfulness, positive thinking, self-care, building a support
network, and developing a sense of purpose, we can
navigate life's challenges with greater ease and develop a
deeper sense of meaning and purpose in our lives.

REFERENCES

Beebe, S. A., & Beebe, S. J. (1991). *Public speaking: An audience-centered approach*. Englewood Cliffs, NJ: Prentice Hall.

Brydon, S. R., & Scott, M. D. (2006). *Between one and many: The art and science of public speaking*, (5th ed). Boston: McGraw Hill.

Carlson, T. (2005). *The how of wow: A guide to giving a speech that will positively blow 'em away*. New York: American Management Association.

Devito, J. A. (1981). *The elements of public speaking.*

New York: Harper & Row, Publishers.

Fleming, N. D. (2001). *Teaching and learning styles: VARK strategies*. Christchurch, New Zealand: N.D . Fleming.

Fujishin, R. (2000). *The natural speaker*. Boston: Allyn & Bacon.

Gladis, S. (1999). *The manager's pocket guide to public presentations*. Amherst, MA: HRD Press.

Hanks, K. & Parry, J. (1991). *Wake up your creative genius*. Menlo Park, CA: Crisp Publications.

Harlan, R. (1993). *The confident speaker: How to master fear and persuade an audience*. Bradenton, FL: McGuinn & McGuire Publishing.

Hughes, D., & Phillips, B. (2000). *The Oxford Union guide to successful public speaking*. London: Virgin Books Ltd.

Jaffe, C. (1998). *Public speaking: Concepts and skills for a diverse society* (2nd Ed.). Belmont, CA: Wadsworth Publishing Company.

Lucas, S. E. (2007). *The art of public speaking* (9th Ed.).

New York: McGraw Hill.

MacInnis, J. L. (2006). *The elements of great public speaking: How to be calm, confident, and compelling.* Berkeley, CA: Ten Speed Press.

Maxey, C., & O'Connor, K. E. (2006). *Present like a pro: The field guide to mastering the art of business, professional, and public speaking.* New York: St. Martin's Press.

McKerrow, R. E., Gronbeck, B. E., Ehninger, D., & Monroe, A. H. (2000). *Principles and types of speech communication* (14th Ed.). New York: Longman.

Morreale, S. P., & Bovee, C. L. (1998). *Excellence in public speaking.* Fort Worth: Harcourt Brace College Publishers.

Noonan, P. (1998). *Simply speaking: How to communicate your ideas with style, substance, and clarity.* New York: Regan Books.

Osborn, M., & Osborn, S. (1991). *Public Speaking,* (2nd ed). Boston: Houghton Mifflin.

Peterson, B. D., Stephan, E. G., & White, N. D. (1992). *The complete speaker: An introduction to public speaking,* (3rd ed). St. Paul, MN: West Publishing Company.

Pincus, M. (2006). *Boost your presentation IQ.* New York: McGraw-Hill.

Reynolds, G. (2008). *Presentation Zen: Simple ideas on presentation design and delivery.* Berkeley, CA: New Riders.

ABOUT THE AUTHOR

MANJUL TEWARI, A BLOGGER, best-selling author, and versatile writer, is the creative force behind the captivating 'Mindset Mastery Series' available on Amazon.

With an engaging and informative style, Manjul's writings transcend conventional boundaries, enriching the lives of readers worldwide. Delve deeper into Manjul's literary world and discover the transformational power of effective communication and mindset mastery.

Visit the **author's profile on Amazon** to explore the full range of captivating works. Uncover the magic of communication and mindset mastery through the lens of Manjul Tewari's literary adventure.